To End All Wars

To End All Wars

Edited by
Dael Allison, Anna Couani,
Kit Kelen & Les Wicks

PUNCHER & WATTMANN

First published in 2018
Published by Puncher and Wattmann
PO Box 279
Waratah NSW 2298

http://www.puncherandwattmann.com
puncherandwattmann@bigpond.com

A catalogue record for this book is available from the National Library of Australia

ISBN 9781925780XXX

Cover design by David Musgrave

Solar plate etching and cover design by Anna Couani

Printed by Lightning Source International

This project has been assisted by the Australian Government through the Australia Council, its arts funding and advisory body.

Australian Government

Australia Council
for the Arts

Contents

1 Amidst The Carnage

The Extra   Adam Aitken   13
Finnegan goes to War   Roland Leach   16
Red Horizon   Susan Adams   17
My friend, the enemy   Margaret Bradstock   19
Stains   Louise Berry   21
Gallipoli: Gelibolu   Brenda Saunders   22
Last Breath of an Unknown Soldier, at Canakkale
       James Walton   24
Ilium   Angela Gardner   26
At Konopiště Chateau   Sheryl Perrson   31
Travels With My Grandmother   Jean Kent   33
Riding with the Light Horse   Myra King   35
Gelibolu   Daniel Dugas   37
Gallipoli   Martin Langford   38
Signature and Inscription   Sarah St Vincent Welch   40
One of the Old Platoon 1917   Rose van Son   44
Skull   Alex Skovron   45
The Last Anzac   Jeff Guess   47
What is to be said   Geoff Page   49
Parallels of latitude   Gisela Sophia Nittel   51
A Blacklead and Notebook   Lorraine Marwood   53
The Sestina Shot for Desertion   Judy Johnson   55
Villers Bretonneux   Gail Hennessy   57
From The Gunner   Linda Adair   60
The Interchange   Jenny Blackford   64
te hokowhitu a tū-mata-uenga   Vaughan Rapatahana   67
boong*   Willem Tibben   69
What I have heard so far   Bhupen Thakker   70
From Little Akaloa to Rhododendron Ridge   Rangi Faith 71
Before and after – the confidence of war   John Bennett   72
The Hours   Malcolm St Hill   77

The Island of No   John-Karl Stokes   78
Magnolia Down   A T Spathis   79
The Great War   Linda Stevenson   81
Missing in Action (1918)   Raymond Evans   83
breaking – 1918   Mark Roberts   85
1914, 15, 16, 17, 18   Kevin Brophy   87
Into the bodies of poor men   Jennifer Maiden   88

2 Some Form of Ending

Nineteen Eighteen   Jill Jones   93
A Biography of 13   Adam Aitken   96
Let the birds twitter   Lyn Vellins   98
Grandpa alive   Anna Couani   100
Luck   Robyn Rowland   102
Parkinson's   Robbie Coburn   104
Our Grandfathers   Peter J Wells   106
Uncle Mac's Leg   Lorraine McGuigan   108
Cave   Andy Jackson   109
That story I told   Kate Lumley   111
The Grandmother's Mythology   Clare Feldman   112
War Wounds   Earl Livings   114
Gunpowder Stains   Magdalena Ball   115
Other War Damage   Paul Williamson   117
Fox-Hole   Mark O'Flynn   115
Over the Fence   Jennifer Compton   119
The Cool Shade   Angela Gardner   120
Anzacs   Rob Walker   121
Piano Tuner   Ross Donlon   123
after Gallipoli   Kit Kelen   125

3 For the Pleasures Of Treasure

Grandpa's Boys   Chris Wallace-Crabbe   129
Frances Turner and Maria Luisa Alcade González
        at *La Colonia*, Viznar, 1936   Pete Hay   131

After Kristallnacht: a lone voice of protest
    Anne M Carson 133
images of evil; visions of hell   K A Nelson 134
spectrum   Hillary Hewitt 136
Imagining Ezra Pound in times of war   Georgina Woods 137
River, take me home   Nihat Ziyalan 140
Anzac Biscuits   Stefan Dubczuk 142
aged four   Norm Neill 143
The Temporary Men   Leonie Wellard 144
The Home songs   Kerri Shying 145
My Husband's Grave   Andy Kissane 147
Raking the Powder, 1943   Andy Kissane 148
Remembering Hiroshima   Ray Liversidge 150
Shrapnel   David Gilbey 151
Fireworks Night / China   Andrew Burke 155
O Jerusalem   Ann Davis 156
Dien Bien Phu   S K Kelen 158
The Long Trudge   S K Kelen 160
Say Istanbul   K A Nelson 162
The One Day of the Year   Jennifer Compton 164
Anzac Day   Les Wicks 166
My mother's uncle   Carolyn van Langenberg 169
Valence (extracts)   Susan Hawthorne 171
One and Ha'pence   Andrew Lindsay 174
Rowan, on the shortlist for Iraq   Erin Signal 176
Instant History (Gulf War 1)   Richard Kelly Tipping 177
Nothing but sunflowers   Rozanna Lilley 179
On World Stage   Yota Krili 180
TV Doco, 2012   Richard Kelly Tipping 182
The Redactions   Kevin Brophy & Les Wicks 183

4 Peace?

Cento for remembrance Dael Allison 189
Manifestly Matt Hetherington 191
Anzac Ceremony 1983 H Isil Cosar 192
Prayer Mike Ladd 194
Report from the Lowland Alex Skovron 196
Asylum Saba Vasefi 197
Weapons Antigone Kefala 198
Wars Jeltje Fanoy 199
The Lord of War Afshin Soleymani 201
Traveller Hidayet Ceylan 203
Fringe Network Anthology Launching, Herbarium,
     Botanical Gardens komninos 204
'vision of the heart' (*ru'yat al-qalb*) Christopher Konrad 206
Away from war Jill McKeowen 207
C * Ç = C Servet Kördeve 209
Mathematics Geoffrey Moyle 210
Kindling Charlotte Clutterbuck 211
Un-singing Mary's song Anne Elvey 213
Some Wars Chris Mansell 215
The General Becomes Chris Mansell 216
A line of peace might appear Anne Kellas 219
Gratitude John Brinnand 221
Missing Eve Gray 222
With Jacqueline du Pré Kathryn Fry 223
The Kingfisher's Wings Martin Langford 224
sounds of stones Kathleen Bleakley 227
Who remembers? Nihat Ziyalan 228
It Always Gets Me Danny Gardner 230
In the Year of Our Lord Slaughter's Children
     Philip Hammial 231
Trench Art Kathryn Hummel 235
This Old House Jan Dean 236
You Stole My Childhood Seher Aydinlik 238

Before and After War   Seher Aydinlik   240
Great Wars   Richard James Allen   241
A Bombardier on the Bus   jenni nixon   242
On Reading Geoffrey Robertson   John Carey   244
The Cenotaph   Katrina Larsen   245
Slow Walk Home   Carclyn Abbs   247
The Politics of Entry   Renee Pettitt-Schipp   248
The Will of Water   Renee Pettitt-Schipp   249
granary   joanne burns   251
Remains the Same   Jill Jones   252

Notes On Contributors & Acknowledgements   253

1 Amidst the Carnage

The Extra

for Billie Sing, Chinese-Australian hero, Gallipoli

Proud, I understudied you, Billie,
tame model minority hardworking &
civil, didn't do anger or shout,
no doctor had to fix your face.
I could play Ned Kelly's brother, but
too Chinese to play you Billie? So they said.
With the metal I wore same or different I
hadn't felt at home with the tough-love script,
how to be lovable in a wrought iron weskit.
It was hard pointing a gun at the bank manager
when I needed a bank.
I stayed cool with the cops in my town
who'd ask trick questions. It wasn't me officer, it was Kelly.
Before the Real War I practiced
self-description, though
no employer deciphered my job.
For the film-shoot a blacksmith put me together
just in time. I shot robotically, so they said,
like it wasn't personal.
The wounded all fell to the ground.
It was bloody.
The ground itself, the whole country cut to shreds.
The director was pleased.

Better as civilian I made runner up
for a Small Business Excellence award.
One year I edged out a calculator made in a dictatorship.
The boss commended the innovation,
my one touch charm control (well ahead of my time).

Then the old matter of my face: too hybrid, not distinctive?
Like all the other faces I'd seen in the camp?
I heard a voice, a ghost's: *Patience child, old actors all retire.*
Your face, all that remains to be done is done.
The dead will care if you care for the dead.

I channelled the haunting and impressed the fresh new panel,
smiled a lot and took a pseudonym:
I'm Ned from up north
and I don't do Unemployed.
Always the first member of the B-team
drinking in the A-team bar.
I was productive, made a good roast duck fried rice.
My grandfather rode in the cavalry, brewed beer.
Mayor of the city, rich progeny.
At the robbing banks bonding exercise I felt
secure, in body armour (iron with velcro buckles)
and after the ambush the supervisor
shouted the hostages free drinks.
Strengths? At Gallipoli I bowled a long spell
under mortar bombardment. I was Billie Sing
shooting Turks by the hundreds, brave but hardly suicidal —
no human wave bullshit, the Bravery column
squared the Common Sense column.
Weaknesses? Who needs to know?
One day I would take a mystery role
for the director was bound to need a big speech
for a dawn service on a distant beach
and a song for the nation's soul
incarcerated in a Dardanelles mist.

I wrote your caption in a police museum.
I was trying to fit, the cute translator called me stranger.
There were realer versions and truer understudies
who knew how to beat up a man and run up a Union Jack.

The gold was stashed in hills and you knew where.
Yep, they said, you gotta play a thief Billie,
not a soldier, not a billionaire.
Do celebrity.
Cook up a feast when the pub's burning down.
Come home and be forgotten.

Finnegan goes to War

This is our own peninsula war. Lord
Kirkmount – make a mountain out of a hill,
a cathedral out of a chapel – said
it'd take quite a few men to take the Straits
but we'd be rid of the Heathens. Then take
the beach – camesawconquered – with boys who knew
beaches. The commanders all British and Sirs.
This is our hill to get up. This is our enemy
to shoot. But it looks like home: same trees, smells, white sand.
We're off to Achi Baba said a hyphenated –
General Sir. We light cigarettes and hope for Christmas,
but the Damntohelles is mined and the ships
can't get through and we're told what to do by prats
in big hats who've never been east of Corfu.

Susan Adams

Red Horizon

1. *Turkey*
The Cove was a mistake. Tight like a funnel
carrying men to their funerals.
Landing in a cauldron of riotous water
blocked by the impossibility of cliffs
there was nowhere to hide from the snipers in hills
bodies became flotsam to waves.
Purchase was rarely gained, retreat was not an option.

Politicians and Gods were the bugles
and both were loose with futures.

No mans land between trenches,
at its narrowest just a few metres.
As each Turk was shot, another stood for Allah.
So hard to win when driven by the call of Jannah.
Self sacrifice an order.

The Anzacs went down outnumbered.
The disarray of doubt and disbelief
spread through their ranks
bodies were stacked on bodies
alive with the dead.
Their legend insinuates our blood.

2. *France*
Memory is a meadow that flows
then grows into the backdrop of every new thing.

It's hard to walk this road.
The flowers keep breeding hope,

yet feet are shod in blood,
the emptied veins of family.

Lie down among the poppies and sticky streams
taste the salt from tears and blooded wounds.
We can no longer hear the larks sing above the battles
the noise of new wars surrounds us.

3. *Anzac Day*
And yet, we mark a day to reflect
on all those dead and hurt
with papavars that grew through bones
in those sun-bled Flanders fields.
The scarlet poppies have black centres
with medals pushed into them.
But pride can't take away the loss
or make it heal.

Part the grass of Gallipoli,
touch the fear still lying in the trenches.
Turn towards the compass points
endings are exponential.

Civilians are the discard of loose moving borders
and families are the sacrifice.
We will not forget,
but let us remember
when climbing on another's spine
we break our own back.

Margaret Bradstock

My friend, the enemy

Gallipoli, 1915.

So this is glory, the chance to die
for your country on some foreign beach
            only we didn't think of dying
but of mateship, the siren call to arms,
to return like heroes, triumphant
            the war all over in a rifle's flash.

Training in Egypt, we knew ourselves
            invincible, repelled a Turkish drive
to cut the Suez Canal, our cannon fire
annihilating distant enemy,
            then partied on like gods, enjoying
good coffee, bad liquor, the women.

Gallipoli was a different story,
part of Churchill's plan to clear a route
            through to Russia, attacking Turkish
defence posts west of the Dardanelles.
But the current took our boats north,
            and the landing was in the wrong place.

The landmarks just weren't there, instead
a vertical cliff rising from a narrow beach
            like an ancient crusader stronghold.
We scaled those cliffs, using bayonets
            as climbing aids, most of our regiment
gunned down in the mounting. The Generals,

Bridges and Godley, recommended withdrawal,
but Hamilton replied, *There is nothing for it*
but to dig yourselves right in and stick it out.
   So we did, digging trenches, building walls
of sandbags, lobbing grenades across this arid
                              no-man's-land.

A ceasefire gives both sides the chance to bury
their dead, the stench of decaying corpses
now unbearable. Soldiers from both armies walk
   together, searching for living men among the bodies.
We can't talk each others' lingo but exchange names,
photographs of wives and sweethearts, share a cigarette.

Johnny Turk is not the fiend of wartime propaganda
   just another soldier, as miserable and exhausted
as ourselves. Then the flags of truce come down
and battle begins again. Sometimes we play games
   a slouch hat or Ottoman helmet on a stick
raised high enough to draw laconic fire.

But light up a cigarette at curfew
   you'll get your head blown off.
Lone Pine is worse, the loneliest place on earth.
Like one long grave, only some of us
were still alive in it. By December we beat
           an honourable retreat from this muddle

of indecisiveness. It was cold when we stepped
           into a small steamboat at nearby North Beach
leaving Gallipoli to the Turks. During the subterfuge
of our evacuation, I found Mustafa's wallet trampled
   in battlefield mud, his photographs −
my friend, the enemy.

Louise Berry

Stains

if life is a spectrum
the hills of Gallipoli
dazzle

crimson of the warrior
nestled next to yellow
each stained the grey and green
clothing of the Turks
the khaki of the Allies

blood of soldiers patterned
rocky ground
dyed the foreshore

over time   red turned to rust
yellow blended with empathy
what was once clear cut
blended into tones of grey

now   dreams and hopes pulsate colour
the kaleidoscope reaches the stars
beams back upon the hopeful

Brenda Saunders

Gallipoli: Gelibolu

"I weep but mother's tears: my sons.
Were my sons, bone of my bone:"
                    Dame Mary Gilmore

In every country town they wait, watch
behind lace windows, fear the final news
from Gallipoli. There is no hearse draped
with the national flag, no last salute –
for the sacrifice made for King and Country
No need for cold meats spread at a wake
Absence is now the public face of loss

The scent of rosemary lingers as women
move through empty rooms. Their skirts
shuffle, stiff as crow's wings. A beady eye
gleams from black jet worn at the throat
a healing stone known to hold ancient fire
rekindles the heart after embers have died

Above the hearth, a young man stands
ready to fight for the Empire, his slouch hat
worn with 'digger' pride, his portrait
– father, brother, son wreathed in black

In every Marmara village, old men sit
silently in taverns, watch the smoke rise
from the cannon fire. Travellers accept
ritza and *meze*, speak in hushed voices
of invasion, sacrifice. Thousands of lives

lost defending the Turkish Empire
And the list of casualties from Çanakkale
In back rooms women fear the news

wait for the real war to reach inside
the family, make widows of young girls
They weep, throw off their brocades
and beads, wear sorrow as a dark cloak
weighed down with feeling

There is no coffin to follow in the street
no public place for them to weep, grieve
for a husband, son, the soldier lost
– men buried on a hillside at Gelibolu

Last Breath of an Unknown Soldier, at Canakkale

How simple in the end: to smell the vinegar of an infant's head
this blink: how different to the beginning,
when the whole world collapses
to a baby's cry.
Know the pomegranate cheated
with hibiscus flowers,
and siren ficifolia recruited through
marooned stars falling in
an aureole of shell bursts

(the blue mosque unseen
the famous river past the cliché of artists,
but we couldn't elude the gum leaves
languidly revolving in their own smell;
I wanted to be the fat magpie
lolloping in the greed of water,
where silver eyes so jealously wait their turn)

Crusader's foolish pose of vigil
thrown down on Dardanelles steps
sighted by Hellespont drowning,
this slow breath of nationality
is more than alien imperial tales
adjudicating the division of souls,
sand absorbs the running of memory
those ripple lines of being
lapping anthems to the billeting stanza

(so near that silly point
my fingertips could touch you my enemy
our embarking coronas entwined like lovers,
now that we understand all the secrets
the last notes home in bugle spit
who ever thought of the stop over pyramids
and these trenches in such willing stupidity)

There is space in my sigh for us all

Too scarce now to want to be visible,
sear my heart into the banksia —
my old nose the wasted cone
that stubs the unwary toe.
Our sun had always wanted me
a familiar smudge in any landscape,
captured in stained glass federation
the cuckoo shrike shatters the gargoyles
breaches all callistemon flying buttresses
(I know your name, I know your name).

Angela Gardner

Ilium

after Sidney Nolan's Gallipoli *Series*

I

in the small shallows of midday
he bends to retrieve
fallen colours

slouch hat, bare chest
an emptied beach, flag against nothing
maybe a ship

out beyond the cut-throat rocks

walks the horses back into their shafts,
a ribbon of old picnic race tickets
worn as a shade to his dark face

smoke hazes their position
making the strappers nervous and sweaty
as the horses shift

II

the moment the guns fire
each horse stands
as if backed against bad weather

a range beyond human voice
attempts to hold the sky
to silence

even as it disappears

III

the horse is waterborne — legs kicking
neck a nebula in Andromeda
exploding shrapnel stars

he surveys the drainage
with its naked dead
the cliffs behind roseate and unhelpful

 — it is Ilium unrecognisable

But for the crossfire
the man's languid pose might be love-made
his naked face

untouched

as on a different beach, his lover
before the rain flattened
 — or hit his left side

IV

cockade and plume ragged
the grasses on cold white sand
bend over their work

 — driftwood in pyres

out there the ships are copping it

all the bright days, the burst
as swimming, they faced each incoming hit
of wave

their touching flesh beset
with exhaustion
bodies ripped in streaming light

  — open
washed in blood, adrift
in limp animal-hipped shallows

V

in the act of firing a weapon
he searches for signs of the enemy
for death almost

beautiful

finds his slack arm holding lost shoes
drone and flash in all directions
the sky spilled

VI

into this two-up — unsaddled
the calm young
tread dirty air's comet tail

the pillion flicks aside

one only is capable of moving

faceless, dog-tagged
held crutch and truss
to an armature of metal

they are parts of a gun
oiled to hollow downcast weight
of prosthetic

  — weapon equal of the man

VII

in a moment of quiet entering the water
horse and rider are alert
for a trail of bubbles to surface

even here where rock or water belay
to knife point
the sea's uninterrupted search

the world put in its place
distant, voided, cast into water
a horizon lacking solidity

VIII

they are limbed again, jaunted and weightless
no longer stilted to be heel-hauled
from open bodies of water

at play in some otherwhere

and the figure he crosses to

   — already falling, gone ahead
dreams emptying like cargo lost at sea

the clean anonymous water
and he the sunlit swimmer
shield arm raised

no longer soldier nor anything from home.

Sheryl Persson

At Konopiště Chateau

The guide says: *he had fish eyes*

but Archduke Franz Ferdinand
boundless wealth corrects imperfections
and noblewomen put daughters on parade
      your heart chose
although her class was such
that at the opera you sat apart
      in life — you stood together
against the scorn of glittering crowns
and at Konopiště Chateau
far from nationalistic rumblings
nurtured love and children

The guide says: *he loved to kill*

bored; pot-shotted birds from turrets
took down two hundred in an afternoon
saving them the long journey south
      and here's a photo
you lean against your elephant kill
glinting pleasure in those narrow eyes
and we hear: emus, kangaroos weren't spared
      (I think of home)
you travelled far, meticulous, your diary
tracked three-hundred-thousand kills
the evidence abundant at Konopiště
boasts the best display of weapons in the world

The guide smiles: *he didn't like culture*

yet I see Franz, you were a modern man
central heating, flush toilets and a lift
        but your decorating skills ...
in courtyards, corridors, chambers
a glut of stag horns, fashioned into chandeliers
        and flocks of rigid birds
hang on walls, dangle from ornate ceilings
still Hitler's SS were totally at ease
        in the requisitioned chateau
amidst polished armour and gilded guns
a dozen tigers scattered beneath their boots

The guide jokes: *he loved animals – to death*

and in the family chapel, your motif
St George, astride his steed, slays dragons
you prayed   for what I wonder   to St Hubertus
the sometime patron saint of hunters
        hunter became the hunted, Hapsburg heir
the bomb missed, but not the shot
you kept upright in the car despite a mortal wound
beloved in your arms   last words begging her
        live for our children
only an assassin's bullet returned to Konopiště
very much at home here on display

The guide says: *his death triggered World War One*

        (she likes her English pun)
and in reply   a discordant haunting cry
a peacock living somewhere in the grounds
has sanctuary now, a century on from Sarajevo

The guide says: *imagine if he hadn't died*

Jean Kent

Travels With My Grandmother

Paris, 1916/2011

My grandmother ghosts the *rues* of Paris.
In the City of Light, she's a shadow from World War I.

I follow the black ink she trailed, the thread
of herself she stitched into letters, posted daily
to her husband, still in Egypt, lost in war.

1916. July. Fate gifts her this blissed hiatus,
this trench of calm, which Paris has also slipped into –
new season hats in its shops, the buses just back
on the routes she needs, daisies and bluebells
in the Bois de Boulogne.

The daughter of a draper and a milliner,
for ten days she will clothe herself
in luxuries for a future – visions of gardens,
a cathedralled forest within Notre Dame,
hours of hope and calm ...

You must come here with me
one day   she writes to my grandfather
while anti-aircraft artillery guard the Eiffel Tower

and she window-shops for a few carefully budgeted
defiant purchases to take back to their *humpy*
on the Darling Downs –
a Sevres vase (only 7/6), a paperknife flattened
from a bullet, a little fabric
for baby frocks ...

new luggage as innocent as their first child,
conceived on his April leave.

Each night in Paris, in 1916, my grandmother
ghosts back to my grandfather,
preparing for the Battle of Beersheba.

She stitches their torn lives into a patchwork of promise
one day they must, surely, sleep under.
When I follow her down the same *rues*,
nearly a century later,
she is a mystery, a family myth,
lost by 1927.

Around the Eiffel Tower now: blue battalions
of police – just *Vigi Pirate, Alerte Orange.*
No war, only threats.
In the seam lines of my grandmother's quilt
her Paris history seeds its own blooms.
Here are two daisies I plucked for you ...

In a hundred years they will be
frail as peeled skin,

the generations that followed
flowering fresh – opening defiant, torn parasols
over new shadows in the Bois de Boulogne.

Myra King

Riding with the Light Horse

Five years ago I joined the light horse troop
Creswick we were stationed
sometimes saving the unwanted
the horses
the teenagers
abandoned
because they were not good enough
not fast enough
for the track
or for life's living
on the edge

But when we dress in uniform
parade the streets of Seymour
on Kitchener's Centenary
or trot the Light Horse Park
I see our black armbands
feel heavy the bayonet
dragging my belt
the 90 round bandolier
slinging my shoulder
and I think of all those
who rode for real
in battle
who died
on both sides
abandoned or not
a hundred years ago
on the sands of Turkey
where we were the invader

And so, I know,
I am not riding for Kitchener
nor for war
but for all the fallen
men and horses whose blood feeds the trees
and scrub
of another place and time
far away
from sanity

The Creswick Light Horse Troop saves unwanted racehorses and helps troubled youth. It is not a re-enactment group, but rides in memory of all the men and horses lost in war.
NB: Not all of the horses in the Troop have been abandoned, nor are all the teenagers troubled youth.

Daniel Dugas

Gelibolu

Each mark on the body
is a path taken
or not taken
is a window of time
a battle on a hill
rain in April
Each scar
on the shore of the sea of Marmara
or the strait of Dardanelles
is a memory of shrapnel
a brush stroke of George Lambert
Embossed by life and death
and now immortalized
on a commemorative
can of biscuits

Gallipoli

We weren't fair dinkum
until
we were authorised
by your deaths.

We had an 'inheritance' –
documents – party – and style.

And an innocent's cheek.

But were only a nation in name
till you breasted that ridge.

We had no beginnings –
no lost chalice,
sword in the stone –
nor dreaming tracks so old
we *were* land ourselves.

Till you
bared your chest
for our spring.

Your blood
washed away
our anxieties:
about British prestige,
about lags, and their right to exist;

above all,
the need to tell tales:

about Cain, and Cain's sons,
or the rights of a non-farming people.

No gestures – mere signs – would have done.

There had to be bloodshed –

a hot scree of carnage –

O how can we thank you enough
for your screams of permission?

Signature and Inscription

I slit the uncut pages
the knife in my child hand slips
tears paper edges

the mythology books are heavy, resting on my knees

the name in the front of the books
is my name too, long and triple-barrelled
St Vincent Welch

I wrangle my name as I practice writing
smudged pencil, bruise of ink and school pen

your signature is convoluted, folding around itself
frenzied and flourished, a man's hand

the letters twine and flick

did I notice then as I do now
their fall and curve, the sadness
the decisiveness of men?

Grandfather Basil,
Commanding Officer, 13th Field Ambulance
ANZAC, Egypt, France
... three Hells on Earth

your signature on these first pages of the myths I read
inscriptions from your beloved father
notes

then absence, no more of you
after 1919

I wrote my jagged name here in the 1960s
inside the sturdy top of a pencil box,
here are my aspirations

I am sad for the girl who hoped like this
trembling with stories and words
I shut the lid

a hundred years later I open Basil's war journal
in the quiet Memorial, his familiar writing is small and crouched,
I read measurements calculated from the North Star
scry lists of *Missing in Action* and *Died of Wounds*
here is the same writing as the signatures and inscriptions
in my mythology books

tendrils of time hold me still, I turn the pages
wonder what his stories were, if we have stories at all

he was writing in his moment, not knowing what would happen

I found goddesses in his books, Isis who loved Osiris and put him
back together,
the huntress Diana, Minerva with her shield, the Valkyrie
lifting up the fallen

you tore pages out of your war journal
I imagine an order an instruction written and given
'Here!'
or were these private words ripped away?
I glide my fingertip over rough remnants
the stubs in the journal's spine
imagine their tearing whisper, read

... the shattered fragments of bones
and blackened shreds of flesh and muscle ...

all things are together in memory
chronologies and histories implode

we are collectors in this family
keep everything till it rattles, speak little,
on occasion speculate
then great shaky tales explode
I knew the pall of their telling and their silence
in our house, still they are being told and untold

I can't guess who he might have been
the father, grandfather, old man
that person never existed
don't know if he ever held his son, Basil, my father
I don't know, as death follows, follows us, hollow

Grandfather Basil, you have three grandchildren
I am one
six great-grand, eight great-great-grand
if we could tell you this

the silence in your objects is your family's silence too
fragments of shattered glass from the Cathedral in Ypres
suspended in our hall, lit up,
dog tags hidden in our cupboards

... a continuous bombardment sounding like ten thousand Gods hurling
mountains ...
... horrors of the shimmer and flash and sudden flare at night of
continuous artillery discharges ...

you scavenged, we hoarded
not knowing what to do with what you brought back
the cold hoof of your slaughtered horse I balance in my hand
the coarse wool of your blanket on my skin
your name in your books, now mine,
your words in your journal I read,
   ... *Maggots!!! ... the cold ... the cold ... The Cold!!! ...*
bloodstained bundles of mangled rags ...

... And this is a war such as the jingoistic, claptrap Pantomime could
never imagine ...

if you had lived you may have told the stories
made more
these objects you brought back are hushed

... the magnificent heroism and soundless suffering of man and beast
...

lecturing with your photographs on glass slides
raising money for a hospital
the pain in your heart and the fever rose
you made a child,
you died when he was six-weeks old

you held these books I hold

Lt Col J B St Vincent Welch 13th Field Ambulance, DSO and 1st Field
Ambulance, from his War Journal 1916-17

Rose van Son

One of the Old Platoon, 1917

Lithograph, Will Dyson (1880-1938)

& he bends to his mate
his hands on his knees
just a helmet on a cross
one of many in this field

& he questions with his face
       with his eyes
& he questions with his chin
       with his fingers wide open
& he questions with the landscape

the burnt landscape around him
holds him
still

Alex Skovron

Skull

The memory circles but never lands,
precarious as that cloudless night in spring
during a long, unspecified campaign
that none of us understood.
We'd heard about Thermopylae, Masada,
our chronicles lit up the Punic Wars,
we knew the lore of blood about Gallipoli
and the Levant. Nothing like this —
here we seemed supremely unaware of
where we were, where we were
going to go, what we were meant to do.
No maps, no charts, no battle plan;
simply they'd dropped us on this cursed
mountaintop, this skull high up above a city
whose name nobody knew, not even
our commanders, taciturn, and nothing
of the race or faith of the inhabitants,
whose soundless airships almost every day
would drone some specie of surveillance
over our sanctuary, such as it was, yet
never deigned descending to an altitude
to gun or greet us, or identify themselves,
expose their language, litter us with words
or pictograms, if that was what it took
to make connection with our mute intent —
which must have puzzled, or maybe amused,
a people (was it such?) whose vehicles,
down there below, far as the eye could reach,
moved with no lucid purpose or design ...

Thus had the winter lapsed, without event.
But on that night, when the moon was down,
they ventured, at last, to assail our citadel —
not by a mode of weaponry we could name
but by this ghostly *whisper* rising from below,
growing loud, louder, and then erupting
into a chorus that transfixed me like a blade.
Its memory still circles, claws at my dreams
ready to pierce; yet it never lands. I only know:
the carnage we unleashed that night, the city
we annihilated in our grand, despairing,
barbarous reply, will tarnish for all time
these shiny coins that camouflage my chest.

Jeff Guess

The Last Anzac

May 17 2002
The last of the Anzacs, Alec Campbell,
died peacefully in Hobart last night.
He was 103.
Sydney Morning Herald

He has gone out now
further than the little beach
that dreamed his death.

At 103 the years had not condemned —
but wearied him
he no longer believed being 16

mattered. He never rehearsed it
in words with anyone
and it never became the fixed bayonet

he eschewed in combat
and that had later rusted into a kind of
forgetfulness. 'Gallipoli

was Gallipoli' his only answer to the
countless questions he'd always been
asked that had no answer. Decades ago

he had left behind the damp hole
he lay in with lice and flies;
enteric fever and bad beef.

His memory had gone on unpaid leave
from that winter of gorse swept hills
and the ten metres

of blood soaked ground
they served up at every dawn
after a mean breakfast. And on to

his final morning, he had no allegiances
to history, the war, or anyone:
except himself. And sometimes

through all those years, out of any
connection it seemed, he
would look again on the Aegean Sea

considering it again as he had that
first time, without this past or legend:
so smooth and silky blue; so clear and

cold, so very clear and cold, that
just before you jumped you could look
deep below the boat and see the sand.

Geoff Page

What is to be said

What is to be said
of General Sir Richard Haking
beyond the stiffness of his bearing,

the strength of his moustache?
How is it that in '45,
unlike the luckless Fifth Division

littering Fromelles,
General Sir Richard Haking
died between a set of sheets,

presumably with nurse attending?
What is to be said about
the man who rose with Haig's support,

the man who praised 'offensive spirit',
who knew a simple rush of men
could overwhelm by force of will

artillery, barbed wire, machine guns?
What is to be said about
a man who, starting late one lengthy

afternoon in summer, 'lost'
more Australians in a night
than anyone before or since,

men who only weeks before
had landed at Marseilles
embroidered by the cheers of women?

What is to be said about
that stunt to save the Somme
and cause the Haking star to rise?

What is to be said of what
communiqués would soon be calling
'several important raids'

notable for Germans captured,
'raids' which left a man
as tough as "Pompey" Elliott

weeping as he shook the hands
of one in eight returning from
his 60th Battalion?

What is there to say this year
of General Sir Richard Haking
beyond the lines he wrote himself,

that prosy but revealing tercet,
even as the mangled still
lay crying out in No Man's Land:

'I think the attack, although it failed,
has done both Divisions
a great deal of good.'

Gisela Sophia Nittel

Parallels of latitude

In one version of our story, Gavrilo Princip,
    named by his devout parents after the Archangel
Gabriel, dies in infancy – like six of his siblings.
    In another version he survives, and applies
himself so well at primary school, the headmaster
    gives him a volume of Serbian epic verse.
Roused by his reading, young Gavrilo,
    born into a long line of subsistence farmers
in a remote Bosnian hamlet called Obljaj,
    spends the rest of his life writing poetry.

Then there is the version where Gavrilo follows
    in his father's footsteps and becomes a zealous
nationalist. Expelled from school in 1912 for protesting
    against Austro-Hungarian rule, our promising insurgent
absconds to Belgrade, where he soon falls in with fellow
    revolutionaries – or 'terrorists' as we prefer to say today.
Gavrilo joins their training camp at Vranje but is killed
    while handling ordinance the group was using
to rehearse their next assassination plot.

In a completely different version, Gavrilo stays in Obljaj
    to become a teacher, who falls incurably in love
with Anna, the best friend of a distant cousin.
    The embers of Gavrilo's murderous rebellion are now
slaked by floods of passion for his bride, and nascent love
    for their first child due early in the spring.
In this version, presumptive heir to empire Archduke
    Franz Ferdinand and his new wife, Sophie,
survive the drive through Sarajevo, felicitously seated
    in the second car of the imperial convoy.

Not the fourth, which is blown up by a hand grenade
thrown by the Vranje band as planned.
The intact royal car still stalls after taking a wrong turn
into the street where Gavrilo would have been that day,
ready with a gun, to accept this gift of fate – but for Anna,
who could have spurned him for another, and did not.

And so Kaiser Wilhelm's never drawn into protracted war
by his Habsburg ally. The cousins on the thrones of Britain,
Germany and Russia remain friends for many years.
And Anzac boots don't touch the shores of the Gallipoli
peninsula. Instead, ten decades on, squadrons of retirees
from Australia and New Zealand swarm from buses
every summer to trek the Dardanelles. To fill their phones
with photos they post on social media as proof
of yet another bucket-list adventure: this time the must-see
rugged ridges guarding open and as yet unspoiled beaches
north of Kabatepe on the Aegean coastline of a land
where Ottoman and Islamic heritage live easily enough
alongside western influence – in this latest variation
on our hypothetical narration.

Many of our travellers then fly on to France.
And after Paris they descend on regions like the Somme.
Hungry for rustic charm and local produce, they practise
high school French on villagers, who forgive Antipodean
vowels when asked about the choicest cycling routes
and picnic arbours – locals and tourists equally oblivious
to the treachery of tunnels, and the misery of mustard gas
and trench foot. And the abandoned corpses speared
on endless concertinas of barbed wire, lacing the horizon
of a ravaged swampland. One hundred years ago
in the final version of our story.

Lorraine Marwood

A Blacklead and Notebook

My grandfather, a non-commissioned officer,
lists names of comrades, their service numbers
against articles of uniform and kit lost in line,
those identities traceable now on the Anzac files.

Men who were once plumbers, or farmers
or maybe orchardists, enlisted in country
towns like Bendigo, Rochester
yet shovelled trenches in Gallipoli,
stripped down to wash in the sea after
weeks of mud, gore, insect and rodent-infested
tunnels.

They shared secrets and scars in the reality
of sudden death and injury, yet against their
names are clear methodical headings –
no name article how lost –
It could be a rifle cover, a great coat
a ration bag, a clasp knife, a chin strap
a hat badge, a shaving brush.
Lost in action not issued or simply lost

How meticulous, how necessary
is the ordinary in the panorama
and illogical mismatch of attack and counterattack.

My grandfather tends his men,
a form of comfort recorded on horseback
or casually talking, walking, taking measure

of each soldier's need in a palm size notebook
marbled end papers, graph ruled pages
and clear copperplate handwriting.

The notebook found just lately in our father's
keepsakes,
recording snippets of a war life,
part of a legend
by a grandfather I never knew.

Judy Johnson

The Sestina Shot for Desertion

'There is not a sign of life on the horizon, and a thousand signs of death.
Not a blade of grass, not an insect; once or twice a day the shadow of a big
hawk scenting carrion.'
Wilfred Owen in a letter to his mother 4th February 1917.

You were so young
and happy at first in the trenches of honour.
With no bugle or drum to sound your own beauty.
It's a marvel your singing kept the tune straight.
Going over the top was a fizz in the blood.
All those excited, patriotic bodies

falling over the other decomposing bodies,
unburied. Maggots older than time in the eyes of the young.
Climbing over the top descended to a blood
sport. And you trapped in the hell of those trenches of honour.
It's a marvel your courage kept the bayonets straight.
Some see bullet holes as flesh-roses of beauty

or Owen's 'full-opened sea-anemone.' Beautiful
loyalties face-down, kissing mud. Broken bodies
cleaned up by pure bravery. But history can't keep a straight
face. Not when it comes to sacrificing our young.
It's hunger for violence that lies behind all that honour.
Ask the carrion birds, those dull porters of blood,

what they think of the Great War. How the Hun's blood
tasted no different to our's. How the cruel beauty
of kill-or-be-killed pulls the trigger of honour.
Well, I have sons, and see no honour in piles of dead bodies.
Human nature's a fucked-up sestina at heart. No young
doubt, ambivalence or straight

up compassion. No commitment to incorruptible beauty.
Just endless repetition. Cliches galore. It's up to the young
to break pride's spirograph. Embrace the straight
line of peace, no matter the cost.
Ignore the compulsion to go round in circles of blood
for the sake of honour.

Oust the old men of power who hunger for War,
and then when they get it, take 6 words as gospel:
   young
        straight
          beauty
            blood
              bodies
                honour

then arrange them in 39 rows of cannon fodder.

Gail Hennessy

Villers Bretonneux

i.m. Private Archibald Dickson
36th Battalion   3292

1. The Soldier

He was barely twenty she was almost six.
She had come from Bidura,
a home for abandoned children,
she thought him her brother,
he had enlisted to fight a foreign foe

and asked her don't tell mum.
She did not want him to leave
and so she stole the soap
from his kitbag, knew it was wrong

she hid it under the verandah steps
for was not cleanliness next to godliness.
Without that essential he was,
she believed, grounded.

After six months home service
he sailed for the Western Front.

She remembered the ship
tied to the shore with streamers
that stretched and broke.

2. The Mother

On 22 April 1918 a notice from Base Records, London, Australian
Imperial Forces, regretted that her son was wounded, and further
stated:

*It being clearly understood that if no further advice is forwarded this
department has no more information to supply*

Hope still stood between her and finality.
Until
On 7 May 1918 an urgent telegram
told her of his death.

She wrote in anguish on 20 May
seeking clarification ...
London answered: *In reply to your communication of the 20ʰ
instant I have to state that the date on which he was wounded is not
available. But the latest information to hand shows that he died of
wounds on 4/4/18 (previously reported wounded). No particulars
are yet available, but later official advice coming to hand should
contain further details, and these, on receipt, will be promptly
communicated to you.*

The military authorities finally confirmed on 21 October, 1918 he
had been killed in action on 4 April 1918 in the attack at Villers-
Bretonneux, and did not die of wounds as previously stated.

In those intervening months
his mother had taken his sister,
my mother-to-be,
to pubs all over the State
brandishing his photo
in the hope a returned soldier
would have news of her son.

3. The Sister

My mother was a young woman
in her kitchen stoking the fire
when she felt his presence

neither comforting nor scary
she ran next door to her neighbour
who read the tea leaves

who assured her he had been there with her.
She carried that memory
all her life for warmth.

4. The Daughter

Some weeks
before my mother died
she told me she had felt his nearness.

He had come in a dream
seventy-five years after his death.

After she died, in her personal effects
I found one photograph from my mother's childhood,
a postcard of Archibald Dickson,
serious and serene
wearing his slouch hat
member of the Australian Imperial Forces.

Linda Adair

from The Gunner

prelude

Apples
falling far from failed trees
on forgotten orchards
make bitter cider.

1. Sydney

The motherless boy grew
like an opportunistic weed
in the cracks of the city's pavement

Raised to believe
in 'God, King and Country'
by his maternal grandmother
and spinster aunts, he became
a professional soldier.

Learned to ride,
shoot and parade drill at Victoria Barracks
Skilled with rifle, bayonet, and field guns
inheriting the eye and discipline of the
trooper grandfather he never knew,
the corporal was ready when a shot fired in Sarajevo
blew the world apart forever.

2. The War
On 29 August 1914 John
or as his mates called him "Bert"
joined the
Australian Imperial Force
First Battery
      First Brigade
Mediterranean Expeditionary Force.

An elegant hand-coloured photo
was taken before departure from Albany, WA,
for the aunts left behind in Sydney
Camp Mena, Egypt, was the first hurdle
old hands became undisciplined
as months passed
and rookies learned the basics

Action could not come soon enough
convinced they were fighting
what their medals would later declare was
"The Great War for Civilisation".

But they battled
as much against dysentery
and boredom
as the Turks, their compatriots
in a hell of Whitehall's making.

Holed up with big field guns
overlooking Gallipoli Cove:
Simpson's Donkey
rats,
lice
and the agonies of others.
Then thrust into the hand-to-hand combat of Lone Pine

horrors never shared
seared into his psyche.

Evacuated via the *'Novarian'*
to Alexandria,
by March 1916 he'd joined the British Expeditionary Force
fighting on The Western Front
the now Acting Bombardier was repeatedly
wounded, hospitalised and sent back to the front line
gassed three times at Ypres alone.
Repatriated without celebration
just before the Armistice was signed.

3. Civilian Life

Swimming at Camp Cove
after his Medical Discharge
he watched the troopship 'Orsova'
sail through the Heads and into quarantine.

A civilian for the first time in his adult life
Bert found the pandemic had struck down
a friend who had cared for his aging aunts.
Abandoned by her husband at the first symptoms,
he volunteered to nurse her and the children.
The woman's younger sister
fell for the selfless and handsome veteran
who, unlike her two brothers,
had survived The Western Front.
Together they found
some kind of solace.

Medalled but never supported
stiff upper lip by day
the bottom of a bottle at night

During the first flush of marriage,
the new father fought "Johnny Turk" in his sleep
drove a chimeric bayonet
though the enemy's breastbone
Just in time, his wife awoke
and moved her suckling baby
before the gunner's fist came down.

Jenny Blackford

The Interchange

My mother's family is full of secrets
as Fruit and Nuts is chunky-sweet.
Her father told me solemnly, when I was small,
his own dear dad had died
at Gallipoli — a stretcher-bearer
like Simpson and his donkey
with the Light Horse Field Ambulance.
Charles Clement's head was smashed by Turkish fire, he said.
See the silk scarf he sent from training camp in Egypt,
now worn to holes; here's the tin of stones
from the Jordan River. A blessing.

Clem's smiling face, too handsome in a torn photograph,
the whole family at his mother's funeral.
An infant son is frilly on one knee,
my grandfather's tiny hand on another.
Clem's older brother plain and sour standing tall behind him.
Good Protestants that they were. Clem would not bear arms.

He'd been a saddler, understood men and horses,
and, I found out later, women.
Some hint he joined the Field Ambulance
a bigamist fleeing someone no more fun, in the end,
than my overly-virtuous great-grandma. My mother,
so proud of handsome Clem, is horrified that anyone could think
such wickedness.

For my mother's sake, I stalked her hero grandfather,
searched the battlefield cemetery across the straits from ancient Troy,
so stony-dry above the wine-dark Dardanelles, in vain.
I'd never known how many of those lost boys were in their thirties,

forties, middle aged with kids. Clem was thirty-seven
when he left Sydney.
Somehow, that made the whole disastrous siege of the near-sheer cliffs
and their sad Lone Pine, even more sorrow-filled –
as did the Turks' vast white-pathed rose-garden, so clean,
so bright, packed-full with bones of men
our own forebears destroyed in numbers never mentioned
in school History.

I dug down deeper in the archaeology of microfilm and paper.
Our Clem, it turned out, never went near Gallipoli.
He sailed from Sydney to the Old World,
a Saddler-Sergeant in the Field Ambulance
of the Eighth Infantry Brigade – not the Light Horse at all.
His service record has him marching in and marching out of camps
and field hospitals in France and Egypt: hellholes all, I'm sure,
just not the hell that I'd been told about.
Imagine moving wounded men
by horse-drawn sledges, carts or wagons, anything that served,
from trenches on the Western Front to aid posts,
dressing stations, hospitals in tents or camps or ships.
Soldiers alive or dead, feet lost to gangrene, fingers shot away,
intestines oozing out. They needed saddlers.

More embarrassing, our pacifist hero's
glorious "Turkish" battle-wound occurred in London,
while Clem was on leave from the Western Front.
He leaned out, courteous, to let a lady board a packed-full bus.
It jolted; he fell back. His skull smashed on the road.
He struggled weeks in hospital, even wrote postcards home
about the nurses, warned his wife
that she might have a pretty visitor, one of the women
who'd been doing good by cheering up the sick.
But there were no magic pills back then,
decades before Fleming's golden bowl of mould.

Infection won that battle.
They buried him with military honours
in a damp green graveyard.

Truth was hidden deep, gaze misdirected from a death so unheroic.
But after his years of trudging dying men, who could blame
a Sydney boy for thinking that a double-decker London bus was safe?

I wish I could applaud the forest of faded-orange poles
high-tasselled at Sydney's Light Horse Interchange,
public sculpture bleak as the ringroad it tries to improve.
Even the tassels — manes, perhaps —
are phone-wire utilitarian. It's a step, at least,
though no spectacular-leaping tribute to all the king's Aussie horses
shipped off to the Dardanelles, the army of farm boys sent with them,
and city-slickers by their thousands.
None returned unchanged,
if they returned at all.

Vaughan Rapatahana

te hokowhitu a tū-mata-uenga

we too were there,
                some of us,
belated, begrudged
& shoved to malta first
        — they did not want us in their 'european war';
                            until they lost
their troops.
we too perished there,
                    so many of us,
languished
bravely, brazenly.

chunuk bair; hill 60; gallipoli

māori boys from some *iwi*
chanting *haka* hortatory,
that held the turks at bay,
more than any involute
                fusillade of   fire

chunuk bair; hill 971; gallipoli

        — the whitemen had then acclaimed our cohort;
                        acknowledged us as
men,
yet conscripted those of us who
                        declined to fight their
bloody battles.

chunuk bair; table top; gallipoli

we too   were   there,
mired/in/the/mud,

                    dying, expiring
for a king
                    who could n e v e r be
                                        ours'.

'Listen, listen, the sky above, the earth below, and all the people
assembled here. The killing of men must stop; the destruction of land
must stop. I shall bury my patu *in the earth and it shall not rise again' –*
King Tāwhiao, 1881.

te hokowhitu *– the first contingent of 140 Māori warrior volunteers, sent in*
February, 1915.
tū-mata-uenga *– Māori god of war*
iwi *– tribe*
haka *– intimidatory war dance*
patu *– war club*
King Tāwhiao – Māori king during and after Waikato land wars. These words
were repeated by his grand-daughter, Princess Te Puea Herangi, when the NZ
government attempted to conscript Māori youth, in 1917.

Willem Tibben

boong*

you know   400 of us fought that war
i tried to enlist but couldn't
they knocked back anyone

"not substantially of european
descent"   so i enlisted as indian

i'd lived on a mission   at the margins
thought this war my big chance   that it would
change things   i'd be treated equal

i was   in the trenches   a digger there like anyone
and those of us who fell were buried far from country

when i came home nothing changed
i couldn't have a beer with old mates
i was not a citizen not recognized as human

still counted with the livestock and the crops
unwelcome by and large   a 'problem'

we could not apply for soldier-settler grants
our lands were subdivided   given to white fellas
we were driven off   made way for them

i fought alright   i fought for king   and country
came home   and i was still a boong

* after the painting 'boong' by Blak Douglas (aka Adam Hill) part of
THEN NOW TOMORROW – AFTER THE WAR, Auburn Peacock
Gallery, 2016. 'Boong' from the name of the first recognized Aboriginal
mediator to the colony – Boongaree of the Botany Bay tribe ... (from the
catalogue of the Exhibition, p20)

What I have heard so far

By Charlie, from Griffith NSW. Died 25th April 1915 age 21. No rebirth. Father ran a petrol station. Mother full of energy. Parents met at Catholic tennis

Don't understand it all. Indian soldiers – Vermillion – on foreheads – (dusty) (Red)
My duty (I like) is to be ready at 11 am. My other jobs completed in 1915. Announced on Orange day. (When everything is Orange)
See it from up here (Yellow wattle). (Green). Never questioned orders. (Don't know how to Mate)
I could not speak for some time (lucky to hear though) the calming (Light Blue) you cannot hear. Deep Indigo Blue silence too
Some things I cannot tell you. But be happy in happiness of others (Dad called it unjealous) (The old lady in the Navy Blue hat confirmed it) (She is always right) (She guides)
Folks with the Pink t-shirts – they smile a bit too much – their smiles light up each dawn – Mum is in there somewhere (waking the multi-coloured parrots up each morning) (she loves such joy)
Big Gold Mirror(BGM) is what helped me. "How can you be so cruel Charlie?" it asked constantly
Now 11 am (Time is Purple) (Time is Gold) (Time is White). Time for me to go and listen to "Lest we forget" somewhere – my only task

"light, my light, the world filling light, the eye kissing light, heart sweetening light" Verse 57 – Gitanjali – Rabindranath Tagore

Rangi Faith

From Little Akaloa to Rhododendron Ridge

Gallipoli, Autumn, 1915

It should never have been this way —
for a boy from the Peninsula —

to stand bewildered with a rifle
hard against a hill
on an unfamiliar beach —

with no boat at the wharf,
no smoke from a chimney,
no totara stumps on the skyline;

this
was never the plan —

it should always have been
a simple song of bush
& bellbirds & family;

now, during those long nights,
he will remember a church with carvings
& an open door
& walls made of shells
where he would run his hands,
feeling the warmth of the sun
on his palms.

He is cold.

John Bennett

Before and after – the confidence of war

1

A century has aged since the Anzacs Corps landed at Anzac Cove and British and French at Cape Helles and bullshit has floated downstream since. I've heard that the Royal Navy landed the Anzacs on the designated beaches after all, but that nervous Australian brigadiers failed to advance as ordered and remained stuck. The same happened with the Brits at Helles – lethal incompetence. Helen's breasts, Simpson's donkey and Homer's gods all offer mythic expectations.

From Gallipoli, Troy was a swim and stroll. The Bronze Age coast drew a line close to the citadel's strategic mound at the mouth of the Hellespont. Xerxes, Alexander and Caesar all paid their respects. They were strategists, Churchill blundered. He had hoped to take Istanbul, open a supply route to Russia and inspire revolution in the Balkans. Forget hindsight, it was never on from the go.

The poet John Masefield (who I loved as a child) piloted an ambulance and wrote 'Gallipoli' in 1916 encouraged by the Foreign Office. The Prince of Wales opened this year's centenary commemoration with extracts from the best forgotten best seller: 'As each ship crammed with soldiers drew near the battleships the men swung their caps and cheered again, and the sailors answered, and the noise of cheering swelled. They left the harbour very, very slowly; this tumult of cheering lasted a long time; no one who heard it will ever forget it, or think of it unshaken. It broke the hearts of all there with pity and pride.'

2

The Iliad's first nostalgic battle shows a Greek soldier Diores being caught by a stone that shatters the bones and tendons of his right ankle, perhaps thrown, not even a sling shot used in the ghettoes of Gaza and the West Bank. Diores falls back stretching a hand out to his comrades, but Peirous, the Thracian who had wounded him, thrusts a spear into his belly spewing steaming bowels onto the dusty ground. Darkness veils his eyes and death is strolling in when Thoas bounds up and spears Diores again, this time near his stupid nipple. The bronze point tears his lungs apart, Thoas hauls out the quivering spear then draws his sword and, up close and personal, splits the belly, spilling Greek guts, long and ropey, pale as tripe … and so Diores dies, one of the first of countless young men.

October 9, 2015: 'Israeli troops shoot dead five young stone-throwing Palestinians on Gaza border.'

Hitchhiking to Iran, I was stoned by children in remote anonymous villages past Lake Van. Once, having finally had enough, I started to throw stones back starting a skirmish. Now I guess blood wells from the torn fingers of children, making my soft cotton T shirts and cheap leather shoes. I'm trapped in comfort, it's time to make a move.

3

Rokshana, what a beautiful name. Was she beautiful like Helen? Were her breasts as soft and white? Were her lips cherry red? Was her laugh musical? Could she sing you to sleep? Was she a mother? Was she a witch? Was she guilty?

A blurred photograph online retrieves a grey rock-strewn valley in Ghor province, a sweep of brown soil surrounds a hole, a little like an Andy Goldsworthy sculpture, except a head sticks out surrounded by turbaned Afghan men. Accused of adultery, Rokshana was stoned to death. Her head was methodically savaged while her voice becoming weaker repeatedly professed her faith – not last century, not last year, last month. Perhaps language will develop.

4

When the earth was bald rock
before stone became loam
before stones became weapons
before stone became metal

before loam became denuded
before metal became weapons
before weapons became nuclear
things were different.

5

October 9, 1916:

Dear Mother & Father,

Just a line hoping all is well as it leaves me at present. Things are just the same here ... There was one Turk who tried to give himself up the other night and got shot by the sentry. We dragged him into our trenches to bury him in the morning and you ought to have seen the state he was in. He had no boots on, an old pair of trousers all patched and an old coat. The pioneers took him down the gully to bury him and one got shot in the thigh by a sniper in the Turks' trenches.

We are not doing bad for food we got that little present from Lady Ferguson that was 2 fancy biscuits, 1 half stick of chocolate and 2 sardines each. I think I have told you all the news so I must draw to a close with fondest love to all,

I remain your loving son Jim.

Last letter home by Jim Martin, a 14 year old Anzac at Gallipoli.

I criss-crossed Turkey in the mid-seventies wanting to live differently, thought of living there. I had five words of language, but loved the country, its history and the people. Esperanto is not the answer, nor poetry. On a beach somewhere east of Mersin I met an old German clambering the rocks. He was tall, muscular and carried a dagger in a sheath on his shorts. A tanned bicep was tattooed with SS Bolts, the sun rune of lightning. A character from Elder Futhark, the Germanic tribes' oldest alphabet used as a neo-Nazi symbol from the Schutzstaffel. I don't recall a blood type. He hated what Germany was becoming, what Europe was becoming. I was a long haired Pacifist, but he didn't seem to mind being strung out and lonely.

6

The Greeks and Trojans spurted blood fighting over the body of Patroklos. In Homer, grief triggers fury. When Achilles hears his love is dead, his amygdala fires up a scorching rage that swears revenge. In gleaming new armour donated by the gods, fuelled by adrenalin and testosterone he works his superb cerebellum and slaughters Hektor with glorious barbarity. He ropes the corpse of the Trojan champion to his chariot and for nine days drags it round Patroklos' burial mound on a trail slippery with an emulsion of crimson slime.

After all the mayhem, the Iliad ends with a temporary truce — but which truce? Which Troy? Ten cities layer silence through this mound, a palimpsest of burials, war and trade. Battles stalk battles, hearts stop hearts and burials finalise nothing — harvests remain wilting in the fields. Between April 1915 and January 1916, 21,000 British, 15,000 French, 8,700 Australians, 2,700 New Zealanders and 1,350 Indians died — and 86,000 Turks died. almost double. A few weeks later the Battle for Verdun started to accumulate 362,000 French and 336,800 German dead, ending in time for Christmas. Maths is conspicuous, cruel and meaningless. The repetition of blade, fever, shell and bullet is brutal.

Aeschylus king of drama and father of tragedy tracks the Greek King home to his victorious return. Clytemnestra is still choked by the resilience of grief. Her husband had sacrificed Iphigenia to bribe the gods. Euripides asks through Clytemnestra 'Suppose you sacrifice the child; what prayer will you utter, when it is done? what will the blessing be that you will invoke upon yourself as you are slaying our daughter?' Disdaining Agatha Christie's method of poison, she used heavy robes to incapacitate Agamemnon in his bath then caved his skull in with an axe. Literature suggests monsters might exist.

7

Anger is dedicated
Anger is obedient to anger
Anger persecutes and imprisons

Anger excites the lizard brain
Anger pounds the skull and blinkers vision
Anger is a sacrifice and promise
Anger counts the days
Anger whips memory
Anger sails in vicious winds
Anger is an adventure that cannot stop.

8

October 9, 2015: 'Baby boy drowns after dinghy trying to reach Greek islands starts to sink.'

If our bones were thinner, our muscles weaker, our breathing slower and our technology stopped at fire, tragedy would continue. Leander swam the Hellespont every night, guided by his lover Hero who lit a lamp in her tower. Byron gave up the first time, then crossed on breaststroke, chuffed he wrote a self-mocking poem. Byron died of sepsis en route to attack the Turks at Lepanto. He didn't die in battle or drown like Leander, Hero or Shelley, or the refugees washing up in the news on Greek and Turkish tourist beaches, a sprinkling of the four million Syrians in exile.

9

Since the fall of Troy, shipwrecks lurk in treacherous currents haunted not by ghosts of the past but the future. Each year 50,000 ships sail the busiest shipping lane in the world. Oil has been spilt and the ships continue to release contaminated water as ballast from their holds. We are waging war on nature, and this is just one small example. Not even the birds will escape.

Could we quietly introduce a blanket truce into the world? I'm not sure if I'm waiting for an answer from those saying their prayers, singing hymns or talking in Parliament. I don't understand my complacency or the ignorance and self-obsession of our species. We could send out invitations to think.

Malcolm St Hill

The Hours

A tribute to Harley Matthews' *The Day Before*

there is no battle scene here
only the anticipation of the afternoon
and the evening and the ticking hours
before the deformed dawn

as the troopships
passed up and down
the animal-calls of loaded men
echoed across the channel
arms thrust upwards as they roared

the wet-eyed colonel
addressed his men
for some he said
at least their names would live forever
it was not too late
for any man to stand aside

below decks
men together yet alone
no past was real
spoke useless words
a last meal a song a drink

engines like the hearts of men
pounded in the dark
the flotsam of before
drifted in the effortless sea

John-Karl Stokes

The Island of No

After war the spare melancholy
of the wharf toward winter: the island
opening the long view South
the wuthering of gunfire on wind.

Safe in this cold anchorage
you can't hear all the cries
you can't hear all the gnashing
you can't hear, can't hear again.

The Island of No is beautiful
grabbing its own to its own
beautiful at cutting the waters
and repeating the patterns, repeating

the patterns, its blow-hards scraping
the fronds from the crevices under the wharf
toward winter, the waves draining
out to the long view South.

The Island, its stealers-away,
take the light by force;
again, again, the waves must die
singing of gunfire on wind.

A.T. Spathis

Magnolia Down

Yesterday three years ago it was the first of July 1916
But tell that to the boys now gone
Tell it to their Mothers who don't yet know to mourn
Give me a break from this torrent of treachery
Lose the truth of it
Send more to the front
As they do the same

Magnolias heavy and full
Ancient beauty they won't see
Or have their sons climb that tree above it all
As it should be

Can't fake it
Can't pretend as the flowers fall
That time heals the theft
Hell no
God bless those who carry
The memories of playing in the sun by the sea
Waves droll, captive to the moon
Beyond and above to light the magnolias on the wet ground

Of course it is, she tells me:
Empty − but he still belongs to me
His old bike standing in the garage
Waiting to pass it onto his son
Did he know love more than a Mother's

In the old box of photos
We four and Mary from next door
She may have been the one

She's with Frank now
And the baby is coming
Told me she was going to call it Terry
Even if it's a girl

I'll give Mary the bike
He'd like that,
Mum says
Time to make Dad a cuppa
And a little prayer for him
It is Sunday after all

The Battle of the Somme on the Western Front from 1 July 1916 – 18 November 1916 was one of the most brutal battles in world history involving over a million casualties with approximately one third dead, missing or wounded.

Linda Stevenson

The Great War

What was great?
Define great for me, present to me
the multitude of words, terms
of reference, apologetics,
the relentless lists/names
of warriors, their deaths
written down as sacrifice.

I'll read you a thesaurus
of sadness, a history of white feathers
posted anonymously to neighbours,
all the sons of one family gone,
stories of women
who rarely spoke again
after the telegrams came.

Oh, it was great,
as in
inordinate, all-consuming, a golem
from hell, huge beyond telling.
But grand, glorious, fine?
… all these synonyms are given,
rationalized. Do they leave you cold?

Soldiers landed home
with no faces. Symbolic
of featureless war engines,
they waited, in wicker bath chairs,
in rows. Millions
were mashed into mud,
crushed skeletons. Legion.

But it was The Great War, they say.
No, it was not. It was just bigger, and worse,
the continuation of petty arguments
between princes; it arose from small
causes, small concerns, like borders,
blood lust, entitlements,
powers.

"It was the war to end all wars"
No, it was not. It was the precursor
of the next ... and the next,
the signpost pointing to
final solutions, annihilation, to the deep,
deep pit, and the most
outrageous pity.

Raymond Evans

Missing in Action (1918)

Nothing of him
ever returned home:
Not a skerrick.
Not even the pumping aorta
the shrapnel severed.
(Of course, there had been
no guaranteed return ticket
when signing up).

He had never really wanted
to come back
with missing limbs
or without eyes
or a brain gone permanently AWOL
in any case.

And the chances
of getting back exactly
as he'd left
– so spruce and able,
and full of mustard –
were now somewhat remote.

So, as he ran forward
on strong legs
into the bullet spray
as ordered,
he had already
sent his mind off elsewhere,
eyes closed.

And whispering calmly
as he ran
the soothing mantra:
"The Goose that laid
the Golden Egg" ...

As he had sung it
over and over
in that high-pitched,
sing-song voice of his
on those golden afternoons
when his Mother was
still the Goose
on their wild, raucous
'goose-chases'
round the backyard;
and the anaemic sun
up there
the blazing Golden Egg.

Mark Roberts

breaking — 1918

— based on Virginia Woolf's diary for 1918

talk of peace
a tremor of hope cries to the surface
subsides then swells again. one may wake
to find the covered murmur proclaimed
from all the papers. but another infernal
wet day & home to tea alone. now i fear
my fire is too large for one person.

ice
walking across the park a troop of horses
run from one side to the other. the gilt statue
is surrounded by a thin layer of ice which i break
with the tip of my umbrella. through the windows
i see great vellum folios full of italian history
an image which won't survive tea.

suffrage bill
the pipes burst in the sudden thaw
from sharp frost to mildness in an hour
so now no baths.
then comes the news
that the lords have passed the suffrage bill.
i feel important for a moment but then
the printer takes me for an amateur. finally
a round by the river & home to cold meats.

the war effort
one small joint of beef
to last a week

no fat to be had
no margarine
& no butter
sunday dinner
of sausages
& bread
& dripping.

dogs of war
no hope of peace this month. policies
have taken a run in every direction
like the dogs near the river
on a vile windy day.

armistice day
then, watch as rooks
fly slowly in circles, or
how a cloud spreads itself
towards the horizon in wisps.
travelling into the city
for lunch with a friend,
factory walls rise
sheets of grey. & how
sirens hooted on the river.
smoke
     toppling heavily
  over
   to the
east.
so far neither bells nor flags
but the wailing of sirens & intermittent gunfire.

Kevin Brophy

1914, 15, 16, 17, 18

He held a war and several grudges
During those four bleak years, yes.
I know time goes all the time
But time stopped for us then.
A waiting game with consequences
And mud. You would not believe creation
Left so much of it behind.
The enemy was within every second
Word spoken in train, booth,
Redacted telegram, casual greeting.

Four years of it
like shooting guns through propellers,
Which we did successfully, eventually,
Learning the skill from the enemy
as usual.
I know time goes all the time
And won't do anything else
But go on to forget us
Our wars our engineering solutions, codes,
coats that got us through the raids
And worries of those moonless nights
When we stopped and hoped
For peace, the temporary absence of war.

We agreed that would good enough for now
As we hunkered down like students
Preparing for another examination.

Jennifer Maiden

Into the bodies of poor men

Eric Milner-White, army padre and the Kings College chaplain
In WW1, wrote back to his colleagues: 'A continuous firework
of light balls goes up from the German trenches. But most
awesome is the noise. We feel powerless against those
splitting cracks and roars, and dream of the metal
tearing its way into the bodies of poor men.' Back home
at Cambridge and shaken, he stopped the regulation
of compulsory chapel attendance, brought in fragrant,
flagrant ceremony like the Christmas Carols, anything
to give the horror justice, seeing the incense of comfort
as *being* a viable justice, offering something different
to those empowered numb, and dumbed by agony. They
attended at the first treble, were promised no sermon,
a scattering of lessons falling like fire on the wind, the bidding
prayer of the chaplain: 'all those who rejoice with us, but
on another shore – that multitude no man can remember',
reminding now of Slessor's 'enlisted on another front', but
even gaunter: the horror not of the last poem, but the first.
The little treble, shrill as a shell, lit exquisite in a silence
as tremulous as his tears sways down the aisle, bidding
the apostates in to pray, on him the unjust weight of every
man's salvation, calling to him in his diamond cry now even
the multitudinous hordes of the dead, and he can see them.
A 'continuous firework', the munitions, but the very building
here by the most profligate of kings, is an incandescent
catherine wheel in continuity: the arches rise vaginal in their
feathery spinal grace, a fortified trench, a structure that a lord
knows will not hold by itself forever. The other choristers close
in on the treble, like long echoing dying voices. There
was a music in the human cries above the 'splitting cracks
and roars', there was a music to entice back any victim, thought

Eric Milner-White as he witnessed the first stumbling treble
tremble towards his lesson like a song.

2 Some Form Of Ending

Nineteen Eighteen

'I want to let go of the slimy and it sticks to me'
Jean Paul Sartre, *Being and Nothingness*

By the end of the year Claude Debussy,
Guillaume Apollinaire, Gustav Klimt, the Red Baron
and the Romanovs were dead.

By the end of the year Nicolae Ceausescu, Nelson Mandela,
Jørn Utzon, Betty Ford, Jacqueline Susann,
Billy Graham, Aleksandr Solzhenitsyn,
and Rita Hayworth had been born.

The Second Reich was over in the mud of the age, the 'gaga
di bling blong gaga blung', the Spanish flu.

Mud is created by water plus soil, silt, clay. Great War slimescapes
were created with organic waste, empty shells, iron scraps, rotting
flesh, created by politics and nation. How everyone had to stand or
fall.

Which they did, or returned to jazz and suffrage, 'Freudian icechest',
depression, 'cocaine in cornucopia', a 'low dishonest' thirties,
efficiency, blondeness, then ghetto, gulag,
brain-washing, los desaparecidos, rainbow warriors, rendition.

Alles schrecklich.

Everything now had to be novel, innovative, unprecedented or chill.
Everything was to be played to the gods, to les enfants du paradis,
spectacle or subliminal. So 'Dada Dalai Lama'.

There will be too much transfiguration etched into sea and ground,
Nagasaki, the APY lands, Bikini Atoll,
Las Malvinas, the Great Pacific Garbage Patch.

The world will do its dada, blast its cabaret places –
Guernica, Dresden, Maralinga, Bay of Pigs,
Robben Island, Selma to Montgomery, My Lai, Kent State,
Stonewall Inn, Tranquility Base,
Tiananmen Square, Amritsar Golden Temple,
Tahrir Square, Tokyo subway, Belfast, Timor Leste, Bougainville,
Aleppo.

All that mud and ejaculate, 475 miles of trenches,
all the final solutions and the stopped clocks, Year Zero,
'Quatour pour la fin du temps', Y2K, *1984*, Brexit.

These things stayed true. Quickness of viruses – they gather more.
They find more place
and win.
Hierarchy of forms – there are only answers.
There's no place for meaning.
This isn't philosophy.
We ask the questions.
Odour of cleansing – finds your place.
Washes your meaning of its natural mud.
It has order.
It has orders.
Gas – because you must breathe.

And the poem will be like you – the Yellow River Flood, Chernobyl,
Jonestown Massacre, the Tangshan earthquake,
the Six Day War, the Cold War, Tutsi vs Hutu,
Cyclone Tracy, Hurricane Katrina, Cyclone Nargis,
Malaya, Suez, Chechnya, Haiti, Korea, Kabul, the Rwandan Genocide,
Beirut, Bagdad, Darfur.

Sarajevo.

Les feuilles mortes se ramassent à la pelle.

Texts quoted directly or indirectly:
Hugo Ball: 'Gadji beri bimba', 'Dada Manifesto' 14 July 1916
Baroness Elsa von Freytag-Loringhoven: 'A Dozen Cocktails Please'
Mina Loy: 'Lunar Baedecker'
W.H. Auden: 'September 1 1939', 'Funeral Blues'
Jacques Prévert: *'Les feuilles mortes'*

Adam Aitken

A Biography of 13

with a line by Wislawa Szimborska

And so the tour begins and ends
in his grandson's drafty grammar school:
"The North Sea wind blew across the Belgian mud
the flames rose in the German east."
Huddled in memory's dispatch box
Major Aitken buttoned up
his 13th Light Horse tunic.
No disgrace, he'd made it back,
from sniping Johnny Turk
to traffic duty at the Somme
to desk jockey on the Salisbury Plain
signing off on casualties,
supervising bayonet drills.
At ANZAC shrines in Melbourne
he'd pray with Anglican attention
and drink like the rest,
his BWM catching the sun.

I swig a VB, the brand his father founded,
millionaire brewer
who left 13 children
and a will as long as this book.
I think of those to whom
the medals filter down.

13 years after V Day father went to Singapore
and bargained with a waif at Changi
for 13 postcards, "so cheap"
he just *had* to buy them.

His talents were letters, logistics,
advertising copy, wearing suits.
At the Office Party in Bangkok
he danced, quite pissed, in women's lace
then swapped the Major's "lucky" digger hat
for a set of Dutch clogs.

When I was 13 my father left home.
Now I dream of a salt ghost
and recall the correct timing
for bells to ring, the melody for reveille
and other regimental habits
like whistles, or the cordite reek
of explosions, or what could make
the trench diorama more interactive
"when all the cameras have gone to other wars".

I think of how to honour a tattooed grazier
who became an auditor of destruction.
How he went to hell and back again,
like a number 13 horse (better than 8)
running on the luck they say it never brings.

Lyn Vellins

Let the birds twitter

i

There was nowhere
 to sort thought
  from rain.
Memory from faces
  too many faces
   were they friend *no.*
She couldn't stop their voices
  they whispered
   then they'd shout from behind
surround sound voices
  bass in front now
   sit down *tell me*
the way back home NO.
   This constant fog
    walltowall demon days
 she walks in silence
   constantly listening for
    footsteps worried about the path
ahead breaking into a yellow sea
  they will all be swallowed
   tossed hurled.

ii

Her fingers on his throat
  she can hear herself choking
   small bones snap his breath
slow one down
   two his head
    matted in red the rock in her hand keeping a constant tempo

three   limp under her hand the bath   half empty
   four   she
remembers a knife
   the look of astonishment and a feeling of relief utter
   exhaustion

iii
They hang there,
coral
against
the bark,
bare feet
dangling
next to hands
chins on chests
and one head
resting
awkwardly
on a
branch.
She stands
back
admiring
the
prettiness
of the tree
her four
children
quiet for once
and her head empty.

Based on am image: Four killed Roma children tied to tree by their
mentally ill mother after her husband was arrested and her Roma group
dissolved. The murder took place on the night of 11/12 December 1923.
Village of Kobzowa.

Grandpa alive

my Polish grandfather refused to volunteer
in The Great War
said it was an unnecessary war
long before the Lusitania evidence
some kind of understatement
spoke English with a Scots accent
happily contradicted patriotic Aussies
in the town

his father had been teaching Polish
in the Russian partition of Poland
and exiled inside the country
the place was a mess
well the war cleared that up

Stefan age 15
set out with nothing before the war
tripping through Europe
and ending up in Scotland
came under the influence of Bolsheviks
somewhere
in the days of The Wobblies

ended up in Australia
in that small town
where I remember
a pathetic granite wall
with names of the dead
carved and with gold leaf

the lines of Dawe so apt
"the spider grief
swings in his bitter geometry"
about the Vietnam war
and that pointlessness
and periodically, sadly
after Anzac Day or Armistice Day
I guess
a pathetic wreath would appear
wilting in the blazing sun
across from the railway station
where Grandpa, alive
waited in his taxi on the taxi rank
and behind that in the park
we swung on the tall swings
in the cold emptiness

Luck

Fear is no more a crime in war than in peace. Inability to control or smother fear
is an unpardonable and dangerous crime in war and, as it is contagious, must be
treated like any other disease in peace time — abolished.
— Brigadier-General Frank Percy Crozier*

I was lucky, lived through Gallipoli,
sent to France. Kept the faith. Lost something
deep that never restored itself. But faith,
that had to go with you. Belief in command,
that they know the purpose. This gives you strength.

Faith in our leaders, our God, that's it.
Fear is contagion, runs through the ranks
faster than rats spreading plague. Battlefield discipline
has to be maintained. The Brits have it sorted.
Discipline helps compliance.

Still, some think too much, lose their way in it.
Field Punishment Number 1 —
shackled to a frame, regulations tell us
how his legs should be pinned,
his hands. Like crucifixion.

Gangrenous after two days, one lad's hands were
cut off; another soldier hanging near the front line
swung as firing practice for the Germans.
'Deserters' are shot by their own friends.
I don't know why they do that. Officers. Make us.

James Crozier, Belfast boy taking refuge
from the cold wet trench in a farmhouse, fell asleep.
They had to fill him with rum, he could barely stand.
Had to be hooked up on the post like butcher's meat
shot at dawn at twenty-one. I felt for him. He was just tired.

Herbert Burden was an English kid, frightened at seventeen,
tears edging quietly down under his blindfold.
I'm glad I'm in the Anzacs. They're not allowed to
shoot us, but Kiwis, that's OK. That's bad luck.
Victor Spencer was their last one executed.

He still visits me at night. His eyes never leave me.
He was twenty-four, raving, with the shakes,
those eyes turned inward, a blankness in him.
Dreadful. He had volunteered,
Maori engineer in a non-Maori pioneer unit.

I knew him on Gallipoli, blown up at Armentières,
executed by a firing squad that could barely
stand ourselves. I wish the end was simpler.
I don't get this part. But I'm lucky.
Only got the squad duty twice.

*Brigadier-General Frank Percy Crozier, in *A Brass Hat in No Man's Land*
(1930), Republished, Hesperides Press (4 Nov 2008, UK)

Parkinson's

i.m. Jack Coburn

terrifying
these empty days in fixation
not on your death but the way you died
the slow progression of rapture in the body
fracturing images
where the definition of muscle has diminished

in illness experience means little
cannot dictate composure
crossing from your eyes of war
long after the deaths of men you knew in youth and have forgotten
the faithless pulse of scars along the earth
where then your voice reduced to minimal protests for sleep

would rather you had left quickly
the ash palled on the paddocks' edge
from each direction light cast long
so that each blade was clear to you
from your unmoving shell

into seeing a culmination of flesh
the mechanical drag of skin as it tears
the way it must pull the taut face into stillness and the long-drawn
severity

still a strangeness in hoping to find you, before grief
where loss ignited your flight from pain
your eminent resign asked for
the scrawl of your hand distant in mine

all breath pitted against the skull
the separation of body, unresponsive years all
I have left of your name

the surge of blood
trailed off   becomes a lull in consciousness
on your farm where I so often walk

grasses that flow gently
   when all breath expires.

Peter J Wells

Our Grandfathers

They came from the city and the bush;
those grafters and wasters, those drunks
and bible-bashers – in black and white pictures –
short but neat, wire limbed, straight-mouthed

our Grandfathers, tugged on a rip-tide
toward France in the year nineteen-sixteen,
the Third Division led by John Monash,
stationed in London, waiting, waiting

for the final call-up, waiting for himself,
for the powers that be, hearing horror stories
and seeing the wounded return by train;
and their new-found wakefulness sent

some to pen, some to brothel, and some
with time to kill decided to play
a football match at London's green-topped
Queen's Club, and five thousand ex-pats

came to watch, to bear witness
to their grace and joy, no need for bread or fish,
no need for the religious man, even when
their kick was not straight, they knew

this was the game of their lives; and within
six weeks the captain of the Third Division side
would be struck down and those who survived
would find the enemy slippery as a spilled mark;

those men, distant from their wives and kids;
they knew it ended nothing, that stand-in peace;
but none forgot the joy of that game, no,
they never forgot the joy of that game.

Lorraine McGuigan

Uncle Mac's Leg

Twice a day he rubs metho on the stump
flesh blue and puckered like a witch's mouth.
Better than a bloke drinking the stuff
d'ya reckon, girlie?

Thirty years on, still fighting the war; dozing
each afternoon, hunkered down in the trenches
at Gallipoli. He buried both brothers there.

Cursing the tangle of leather straps, the shoulder
harness keeping *the brute* in place, he throws
the leg down one Anzac Day. Beats it till his stick
snaps. And weeps.

Cave

When the wound healed, and the patient was going about with his wrecked
face uncovered, I was sometimes sensible of the embarrassment to which
allusion has been made. I feared, when talking to him, to meet his eye, that
inadvertently I might let the poor victim perceive what I had perceived:
namely, that he was hideous
— Ward Muir, Orderly at Third London General Hospital, 1918

The park benches outside the hospital
were painted blue — code to the locals
to move along, in case a patient arrived.

The one I can't forget had been coaxed back into town
from a cave he was living in. *The woman I love*
finds me repugnant. She has a right to.

Our clinic walls were lined with prosthetic faces,
flags and posters. Not a single mirror.
He told me, *it was a sound like someone smashing*

a bottle in a bathtub, only my own skull
was the porcelain and the glass. What could I
possibly say to such a story? Three times a day,

I pushed a rubber tube down his throat
and poured in beef-tea or milk. Too often
it went in wrong — he'd choke and cough,

then nod, as if saying, *all ready again.*
And still you want to know what he looked like.
His surgeons worked from the inside out,

each layer – bone, flesh, skin – building up
the semblance of a face. They learnt much
through their many failures. As I did

when I looked into his eyes too deliberately.
The air between us, a frozen river.
I carry a shard of it in my stomach.

Some of the patients formed a football team.
We're guaranteed a win – the other team
take one look at us and run the opposite direction.

You might imagine he joined them on that field,
his brokenness becoming only one among many,
and that after the fifteen operations

he filled out the pension forms as suggested,
writing *repulsive*, eventually marrying
a beautiful, gentle woman. But I was not surprised

to see him, as he left the hospital, walking
toward the limits of the town, back to the ragged,
open mouth of that cave, the peace of it.

That story I told

i.m. Pte Henry Russell Prince, MM, 45th Battalion, AIEF, 1896-1954

Then I get to the ending. It isn't neat,
& my voice crackles like a gramophone

record needled with dust, telling the kids
the one about the great uncle they never knew

who dug in near the Dardanelles, and somehow
survived. He returned to another littoral, but

the sweep of Sydney Harbour & clarity of light
could not reconcile the shapes of day with night

& the smell of war lingered.
Maybe that was why he axed his medals,

took his gun in a leaden salute & fired.

Clare Feldman (1927-2014)

The Grandmother's Mythology

I
She told us once. Just once.

They came three times, the men of Zeus
bonded by Hermes to carry the news of war
from Elysium to Darlinghurst.
They could have sent the messages together
for pity's sake to have it done with
but chose to spread the pain piecemeal
as if to savour it.

Came the first into the busy street
sweeping it clean as a plague town.
Mother and daughter, still as death
watch through lace curtains
praying he would choose some other.
Three steps from gate to door.
Missing in action
read the favour of the gods.

Came the second, not granting pause to weep.
And the same fear resurging
holds the women against drawn curtains
praying for the same deliverance.
Three steps from gate to door
to confirm the death —
but of another.

Came the third, short seasons later.
And the women, their dread beyond imagining
clutch at drawn curtains, their prayers exhausted.

Three steps from gate to door ...

HE DIED FOR FREEDOM AND HONOUR

Years passed, and the worst pain over
the medallions reached the mantelpiece
and rested
waiting there above the comforting hearth
until Hermes must again
call up his messengers.

II
Except, except –

A generation later
came Hermes in a different hat.
No messenger this time but sad companion
bringing not noble myth but shameful truth:

"The first one, yes, had died.
Not on foreign, tortured soil
but in his own land.
Not by random bullet
from anonymous foe
but by his own hand
turned inward."

For the women
the message was as cruel
as any other in a time of war.
Their first prayer quite unheeded
that the dreadful cup should pass
and leave them be.

Three steps from gate to door.   Sydney 1915/1917

War Wounds

After a war of dying empires
squabbling one last time
over destiny and honour,
my grandfather toiled hard soil
for a castoff patch of a land
that mythed itself a nation
when its sun-drenched warriors
charged, fell, bellowed and cried
over a spit of craggy land
thought strategic enough
for slaughter.

He toppled titan trees, grubbed out
stumps with shovel, mattock,
sweaty gelignite − my father's hand
swiped across his forehead
fired a headache crueller
than migraine, one more lesson
in a day spent teasing out the habits
of boy and man as they cleave land
for thin grazing.

A weeping shrapnel hole under his armpit
the size of my father's seven-year-old fists,
legacy of Villers-Bretonneux, my namesake
grandfather died of chronic infection,
too fraught by milking and pride
to seek a doctor's easy cure,
too drilled by manhood to foster touch
from father to son, homelands left
for dead thistles.

Magdalena Ball

Gunpowder Stains

In this world, I remember a man
with gunpowder stains
colours indistinct as burns
a reverse pattern devoré

when he smiled the room became
childhood, the cracked memory
he couldn't shake
faded into a line where craft met capability
the simple pleasure of a job well done

he coughed and the world went black
fear became his clothing
a protective cloak he came home with
clinging against hot skin
raging into the morning

the very last time I put him on hold
breath came through the phone
into the room, while I just listened
for something that couldn't be
put into words, the stutter of war
the flinch, somewhere in the past

that scene grew in my mind
vivid in emulsion coated negative

I knew the explosion was imminent
there was no weapon that might
track that sound

all those beautiful boys
crying for what they couldn't unsee

no truncheon would break the
thin thread of hope holding him
on the line like Schrodinger's Cat

holding back the heather sprig
of loss that slowly, finally
broke his heart, the beating just
stopped mid-sentence

while I waited forever
fingering the telephone
constricted and shoulder flinched
for detonation.

Paul Williamson

Other War Damage

The drunk gave the curly haired infant a silver coin
as he sat well-behaved between parents
on the park bench. They were tolerant
respectful, even though slightly worried.
It was the child he could not have
with what the war had left of him;
or if he had a child like the veteran father
the one he could not live with.

The football field was unarmed combat.
Two ex-soldiers finished the playing life
of an opponent in seconds.
After the game they had a drink
not thinking about the one stretchered off;
it seemed a fairly normal battle.

Fox-Hole

Two men and one fox-hole,
the old woman who knew him said.
Two men and one man-sized fox-hole,
ordnance shells flying overhead.
One fox-hole, two men working hard

now only one man, a young man, my grandfather
buried alive at the bottom with the foxes,
hard work digging him out, the other
boy blown to bits on the chalky, fox-holed shore.
When he returned to Ballyhaunis

hunting pine martens, a red setter at his side,
the old woman called him 'that terrible small man
wheeling a bicycle, came back from the war
didn't do a stitch of work for six years,'
not until the wounded boy inside him died.

Jennifer Compton

Over the Fence

Thinking Of The Call Out For The Anthology For Gallipoli
I Realise I Never Knowingly Met Any Of The Gents Who Were There
But I Knew Plenty Who Were Somewhere Else

So long ago. I was a little piping child.
I don't remember how I got over the fence.
Great-Aunt Mary was mowing the lawn
– ratchet ratchet ratchet went the steampunk mower –
Great-Uncle Frank was collapsed like a marionette
legs in front (one of them not natural) and bent
to cough and gasp, grey in the face, a misery to himself.
(He was gassed.) (Dulce et decorum est.) (Now I twig.)

On this occasion, this one time, before he died young
he smiled at me. I shimmered up towards him
like a daisy that has learned to walk, and tapped
his unusual leg (trousers rolled up). "What's this?"
I asked. "That's where they took away my leg."
"Why did they do that?" (A curious and trenchant
child.) And then the long, slow, five miles wide
smile of experience cherishing innocence.

Angela Gardner

The Cool Shade

Those commemorative avenues, an equation,
one life for another

how upright are the trees of an emptied country
town in Summer

the browned land falls to dust, occasional clouds:
water towers vaporising in the heat.

Into the hot burden of a day: squabble of birds
sticky residue of flower and fruit-fall.

I drive into and out of each town through arcades
of light and darkness

Those long dry avenues of sun and shade,
sun and shade. Sun

and shade.

Rob Walker

Anzacs

and when he came home from the war at
21, walked back to the familiar laneway
between his little cottage and the factory
in Trembath Street Bowden dad left a
lot back in New Guinea. he married the
woman he loved became a cabinetmaker
had two boys and lived in a redbrick war
service home in Richmond

never worried about the RSL the
marches the reunions rarely spoke about
those years would rather do a crossword
than have a cross word or drink with
old soldiers preferred reading a book to
joining an anzac march when I asked
him why he said that was then and this
is now

and when my grandpa came back from
the so-called Great War with an ugly
stomach from shrapnel and only one
wheezy lung from mustard gas he went
on a TPI pension because for the rest of
his life he could only ever do Light Duties
and when I asked about his wartime
experiences he said war's bloody stupid.

so I don't understand how anzac day has
grown into a quasi-religious celebration
in 2014 and all the talk of Sacrifice
and Honour and Respect is used to

justify subsequent wars and invading other countries or in the same week that our prime minister sits in a fighter jet beaming like a boy with a new toy he says 145 million will be spent next year on the centenary celebrations and by the way we may have to cut pensions.

Ross Donlon

Piano Tuner

i.m. E.G.L. (1896-1929)

This is a poem about the gaps in a life,
the what we don't know about someone
in their dash (–) between birth and death.

Sent back a cot case, he never returned
to Murrumburrah-Harden, the slap-dash
town on two hills, creek in-between.

Not even for his mother's funeral, they said
when the wattle and daub life killed her
after service on the Domestic Front.

He was *raised in a hard stall,* they said,
known around race tracks as *the runt,*
the jockey or *the rabbit shooter,* that's all,

so why wouldn't he get up and go,
take off when a parade and drums
thumped glory down Albury Street?

He'd *See the world. Roast Turkey,*
but ticks on a clipboard showed more.
The rabbits trained a marksman.

14th of April 1918. Mont de Merris
gallantry under fire wins the Military Medal –
'the other ranks' Military Cross.

Wounded but not enough, he's sent back
to the front. Shot in both knees. A boat
with crutches brings him home to no one.

But War, never ready to end with Peace,
follows the soldier like a jealous partner.
Their reunion in Tumut kills him.

Well known locally as a piano tuner, an obit
says off-hand. 100 years later, the odd phrase
tinkles curiously over gaps, hard to understand.

From convict's grandson to Military Medal.
Shooter, clerk and physician to pianos — facts
strike discordant notes as to the sum of the man.

In convalescence, he'd embroidered a rising sun.
Long gone now, it once seemed a feminine thing,
but nearest to his touch on a piano, that delicacy.

after Gallipoli

voice of the soldier settler

the hey dad years are all away
and now the work's

among trees of my truth
each animal telling

you could be with them some days
down the back I mean, where it's scraggly

all up with the sky, you could imagine
we were the first ... that no one had ever lost this land

you'd think it had drifted to us in a dream
as in when we weren't looking

God, why are we here in paradise?
why must we leave so soon?

nowhere to go but that single uncertainty
one proof lacking against all that is known

in the orchard, at the place of the fountain
sweet waters run with the stairs

a trench for blood and the ghosts will come
all these years from Ilium

the war still in your head
look up through branches so you see

we followed orders
brave death we are

isn't this any-sky our flag?
all unfamiliar stars

because our skins
are like a song

and that was just the trouble
how we were faithful to a fault

and couldn't see the you for me
but now — as one ghost to another

let us sit to tea together
I haven't got your language

I read your face as you read mine
take my hand, take your end

of the conversation
we won't have need of words

3 For The Pleasures Of Treasure

Chris Wallace-Crabbe

Grandpa's Boys

Garrulous and footloose, a little chancer,
he had once been Scottish, wrote stuff about it.
She had sailed out south from Cork
with bloodthirsty blood in her girlish veins.

He lived here and there, much like Zelig,
but she hooked him in drowsy Adelaide;
they lived in three or four cities
practising his reinventions pretty well.

The boys were got, briefly, into good schools
till the fees were called for. Their olive sister
became a teacher, first of all,
while Keith worked clerking for Hutton's Hams.

But now a giant war came rumbling along
so the latter dropped his steel pen, sailing off
to pyramidal Egypt. Nobody knows
what his father was thinking by now,

the personal diamond mine only a memory.
Keith was shipped into the Dardanelles
to die in bloody dust, a hundred years ago.
Dad was meant to avenge him,

their mother swore. She was more or less tribal
for a tiny lass, but Kenneth survived
to rollick and sweat through a new global war:
this time in Asia – once reported as dead.

Burma had merely fed him shrapnel incisions
and after them he took up his own steel pen,
typewriter rather; camera would be his choice.
Based for years in Uttar Pradesh,

he managed to over-fly that continent
between architecture and propaganda,
his life rich as curried goat,
fragile as pale-blue aerogrammes.

Through all that global arkus-malarkus
my father strutted in warm style,
devoted to young me, yet
nimble and garrulous like his old man.

Pete Hay

Frances Turner and Maria Luisa Alcade González at *La Colonia*, Viznar, 1936

'At least two women lived at La Colonia *... It has not been possible to trace either of these women'* (Ian Gibson, *The Death of Lorca*).

It is easier to picture Frances Turner —
as an English rose, strayed lucklessly
        to the maw of hell,
though the blush of her cheek,
her wave of chestnut hair
        are more apparent than her politics.
Whatever these, she will yearn
for the sedate lanes of home,
        will set herself this goal:
        to endure.

      *   *

Maria Luisa was comely, we are told,
        and prominently of the Left.
How well did she lie in the bed
        of Captain José María Nestares?
What unfathomable windings brought her at last
to the curve below Viznar's white walls
        and her protector's pitiless bed
        in *La Colonia* of the doomed, last lodging
        for the killing fields of the *barranco?*

It cannot be imagined –
yet some resolving *must,*
      and it insinuates …

In my spinning of it, Maria Luisa
      looks down on the olive grove,
      her back to the *barranco.*
She is preparing the last meal
      for the next condemned detail
      of lost and silent comrades, her friends.
She spices the *tortillas* with salt tears
till the *barranco's* thunderous report
signals the slump of the newly dead,
      the yaw of the pit,
      its shapeless, tumbled meal –
fit to receive, too, the remains of her own,
      lovingly, last-night prepared.

        *   *

Were Frances and Maria Luisa each other's comfort,
or did they pad the halls discreetly,
      each silently where the other was not?

Witness to such atrocity,
do they, too, lie nameless and bullet-punched –
      even here, perhaps, in the Viznar *barranco,*
      one with its shapeless ghosts?

Let it rather be that they chose to lodge
within caves of time that baffle light,
      there to hold their secrets
      close unto death.

Anne M Carson

After Kristallnacht: a lone voice of protest

Melbourne, Australia, 1938

Resounding silence inside Germany and out.
No word from neighbours, service clubs,

churches. No government anywhere in the world
utters even token protest. How the Nazi brass

exult to have got away with so much! One lone
voice rings out: 78-year-old Yorta Yorta man,

William Cooper, delivers a petition to the German
Consulate in Melbourne. Permitted through the gate

and up the steps, halted there – the Consul refuses
him entry, refuses to come out from behind

his door. From one persecuted people to another,
William Cooper speaks across continents directly

to Herschel Grynszpan and the millions to follow:
I hear you, I see your suffering, you are not alone.

images of evil; visions of hell

... in nineteen forty three
Tucker brought war torn Europe and modernism   home
to the streets of Melbourne

talk about dark
          dark night of the soul   baby
dismembered bodies reflected
          in the headlights of trams
predatory men
visceral women
surreal cinemas
          made for a very ambiguous canvas

his leitmotif: exaggerated mouths
          Bright Red
                    Crescent Shaped

nostrils breathing smog and gunsmoke

he put a big question mark at the end of   normality

brought home
stale bread
sour milk
mouldy cheese
          fucked all   the staples

it wasn't pretty

Come the new Millennium
visions of hell

migrated   from

Iraq

          Afghanistan

                    on   w I d e   s c r e e n s

PTSD: the new staple

spectrum

He leaned over my easel and guided my hand into buttering strokes of
Flake White – lead based, traditional, the toxic glisten like snow on my
No 8 bristle. I thinned with oil, breathed linseed as I built up layers, fat
over lean, thick over thin, each one more flexible. I studied the model
(fully-clothed, one hour pose), saw how the cold northern light threw
the old woman's face into shadow – cloud at the window – the sheen
on her collar and hair; watched Jakob stipple lace with a fan; learned to
highlight with Titanium, the brightest yet most opaque of the whites
(Cremnitz too stringy). In spring, when the leaves of the plane trees
that bordered the Seine were dusted with cream, he showed how a cool
touch – Zinc White or Lemon – could slow that hurry and growth. All
summer we wore down the warm yellows of sunlight and stone, blocked
fields and houses, crimped each tube to the neck. As evenings turned
indigo I moved to lavender hues; *Still-Life with Two Glasses, View Past
Open Shutters, Shadow on Nude*. Rose Madder and Carmine were my
perfume. Our palettes darkened, converged into Umber and Earth.
Poland burned in September. Jakob rushed home to Paris. I caught the
last train to the coast, my canvases crushed beneath mess kits and army
great-coats. Payne's Grey, the slate mountain of water and cloud, a boat-
load of stragglers hell-bent on Dover. Black captures light, draws the eye
in like the glint of a uniform badge, or a gun. The coarse tone of Carbon.
Graphite's metallic. Ivory Black, gritty, made of charred bone.

Georgina Woods

Imagining Ezra Pound in times of war

Among the smiddereens,
a shard, this fragment, careens
from the epicentre of the blast.
Out, out, the pieces are cast.

The Blast: 5 June 1915

Partridges jog above the trench. In his pocket,
Gaudier-Brzeska fingers the carved butt of a Mauser
rifle, and Ezra's new volume of old poetry.
Tomorrow, he will lead them to the Labyrinth.
He reads to the company with fervour:
Lonely from the beginning of time until now!
Bones white with a thousand frosts
Who brought this to pass?
Who has brought the flaming imperial anger?
Each foot of soil won by the French is bought
with whiteness: bone, empire, frost, ashy
residue of a blood-thirsty young sculptor:
"I have been fighting for two months
and I can now gauge the intensity of Life."
He was one of several thousand victorious
French who died in those muddy weeks.

The Cage, August 1945

There is no burden like error: an old man's fasces
borne on his back. The wreck of dead cities litters
our children's path or buries them, faces ashen grey
with tower-dust. Rain carves dribbling waves down
the hoary head of the poet: culpable, forbidden rest.

The poet was safely seized when the Little Boy made
the city of peace — scattering words and cranes.
All the fragments released their hands, and dropped
their bonds in relief.
Wave and wasp flew out
from the blast. A scientist watched the *pika*,
the brilliant light, collecting data and composing a letter
to his little boy, about the peace of terror, while Ezra
laboured over penitent and tender cantos. His vast poem
omits this crowbar thrust into our deepest vortex,
jemmying open the cage and unleashing the captives.

The End, November 1972

One hundred years of mud and ash mashed in jar,
painted and carved with friezes of frozen cruelties,
immortalised vanities. Kissinger thought peace
was at hand, the week Ezra died, with many others.
"Human masses teem and move, are destroyed
and crop up again. Horses are worn out in three
weeks,
die by the roadside. Dogs wander, are destroyed,
and others come along."
The jar is open. Who brought this to pass?
Ash begets ash. There's no cause, at the last.

Coda: 2015

A woman is dragged by her hair to Nauru across
the newspaper, above the island President's letter:

> *Cosi vivere che I tuoi figli e i*
> *loro discendenti ti ringraziano*

The stones turn and turn. A dusky patina settles
with a rustle like the shivering wings of a wasp colony.
We sift through the dust, entreating each other for pity,
now that we have turned the rock over to answer the mystery:

"how could anyone let this happen?"   Just so.

This poem draws on source material from Kenner's *The Pound Era* and the
poetry of Ezra Pound.

Ezra Pound, "Lament of the Frontier Guard." *Cathay*. 1915.
Henri Gaudier-Brzeska, "Vortex: Written from the Trenches" *BLAST*.
2 July 1915.
Luis Alvarez, letter to his son, written aboard the Great Artiste: "What
regrets I have about being a party to killing and maiming thousands of
Japanese civilians this morning are tempered with the hope that this
terrible weapon we have created may bring the countries of the world
together and prevent further wars." Quoted in Rotter, Andrew. Oxford
UP 2008. *Hiroshima: The World's Bomb.*
Henri Gaudier-Brzeska "Vortex: Written from the Trenches" *BLAST*. 2
July 1915.
"Live such that your children and their descendants will be grateful to
you" words Pound printed on a poster for distribution in Rapallo. Cited
in Hugh Kenner, *The Pound Era*. 468.

River, take me home

I'm contemplating Parramatta River
in Sydney
my life, clear as water
flows by

In '99, on Istanbul – Taksim Square
the brotherly kick of Özdemir
how I evaded it, in kind
the smile of witnesses
to our childhood joy, all in the stream

A fish jumps
flicks its tail
without taking its eyes from me

It reminds me of the fish
I caught by hand in the Seyhan River
I tried to keep it in a jar
was scolded, released it back into the river

Wait a second, Parramatta River!
I'd like to have a word
with that fish
Have they gone or still waiting for me?
My loved ones, whose funerals I couldn't attend?

The sparrow who joined me
and shared my sorrow by the sea
the fish that stopped and waved its tail at me
I know them all from my birthplace Çukurova

Are you taking them where they came from?
While carrying everything away
don't leave Nihat here, river
take me home.

Stefan Dubczuk

Anzac Biscuits

A dream then, stacked
in thin tin, *J & E McD* scratched, glinting a billy
tea lid. Muddy as porridge when ground down.
Dried: the shape, colour and weight of cow-pats
in our back paddock back home:
golden

syrup, rolled oats, butter slick on Mum's
sugar-white palms guiding my pock-marked
bi-plane home —
fingertips clip-clipping still

-green ears, bank to strafe the chooks
a spray of pellets, circle the water-tank tower
(twice), heels parting grass, taxi the back veranda,
buzz yet another blue (the blowfly dogfight
slapping our back door), duck Mum's sweaty
hangar arm —
halt —

chocked, before

Dad's empty chair; brimmed milk-glass warming,
golden bake-tray cooling, on the kitchen table; home,
safe from another perilous mission: *The Attack
of the Black Parrots* —
daydreaming

past

I'll fudge my age, enlist, for my country
needs me; bunk up with big brother — *the boys:*
Jock on top and me on the bottom, at last
light. Sleepless, sharing voices, laughter, noises
in the dark. Flicking scraps of biscuit
as shrapnel.

aged four

Windlesham, England, August 1945

We didn't really know what war was; we just presumed
that everybody had one. We weren't quite sure which way
was east or west but knew exactly where the planes
that grown-ups called the bombers flew. We listened
to the sirens wailing in the nearby town and counted time
between the bangs. We didn't understand why people
said we shouldn't wave to soldiers dressed in long grey coats
passing by with others dressed in brown and holding guns,
and did it anyway.
      According to the time of year,
we built fat snowmen, danced around a maypole, plaited
daisy chains, picked blackberries on the edges of a field
or jumped on piles of swept-up leaves. And then one day
the bangs and wailing stopped and men appeared in houses
where they'd never been before and children had to call them
dad. We grasped that life had changed, promised to be friends
when we were sent to school and, in our special corner
by the chestnut tree, we talked about the good old days.

Leonie Wellard

The Temporary Men

The ships are leaving for Europe.
    Cargoes of men jostle on decks
        to glimpse a face.
Lungs steal the salt air
    then give it back on words falling
        to the docks below.

Women net their hair
    and start to carve a different life.
        Under their snoods
these temporary men
    from kitchen, laundry, nursery, anonymity,
        don overalls and boots;
drive trucks and buses;
    harvest crops; become butchers,
        electricians, welders, plane assemblers.

Farms and towns maternalise;
    factories attune
        to lighter voices;
machinery of every kind runs
    just as smoothly
        to the coax of female fists.

It seems Australia rises higher on the sea:
    so heavy is the weight of men in their leaving,
        so much lighter the country
with their loss,
    as ship after ship
        slides gently down the horizon's throat.

The Home songs

5. Running home, running home

Poppy used to put both feet inside the laundry basket – sheath his
body in the coats hung on the doors for extra warmth at night – hide
from the MP's – yes here they came again for his absconding arse –
small kids answer – too easily – he's there, she said – he never did go
to war – he was in the military prison the whole time – nobody says
good on him – wouldn't shed blood for those English mongrels –
they say coward lazy man – Nanna went to visit him – he ran every
chance he got – always ran home where they traipsed sighing off to
catch him.
He called his medal-wearing counterpart digger – adults flinching
in the car on the way home – it would be why I remember but I
never saw a motion of it between the men themselves – too small
maybe – too small. We still loved the fucking coward and the busted
and the broken we loved them couldn't leave them – couldn't pass
beyond that wall – never looking back or down on memory's habits
styles and foods – nothing just ground zero and a blackbird's eye for
gathering the new.

Three Hats

1.
First their father went far distant – turned to paper sand and letters
– mum grew larger closer – shifted into spaces called the War effort
then the effort took them all

2.
the children taking care to gather tinfoil – aluminium for aircraft
all must make the effort – I got a photo the other morning in the
post – my father and his brothers all lined up – tin helmets at their
feet – beside them tall and languid, dark as molasses their mother –
living with them all in one room – fair game – darker game – now her
husband was away – renting out the other rooms – getting by the best
she could expanding into all the places parents had to be

3.
What happened when disembarkation came – the men inserted – she
shrinking back bit by bit – to be the hard and tensile steel the children
all remembered – tough women then surplus – army surplus – men
surplus – children broken shards of family – should have taken up the
hats – put them on not thrown the things away.

Andy Kissane

My Husband's Grave

I ripped a cotton thistle from the grass beside your grave.
No doubt you stepped on them on your last march,
pulled the spines from your trousers, admired the lovely
purple flowers. How far you walked, past burning haystacks
and deserted houses, past women who looked at you
and looked away. I'm sure you dreamt of the shady verandah
at home, bees flitting about the garden, my plum jam cooling
in the kitchen, a long letter safe in your overcoat pocket, a poem
written on the back of a handbill advertising cod-liver oil.
Your dear friend, Miklós Lorsi, was shot beside you,
the bullet slicing into his chin where he once rested his violin.
If you'd marched with the second unit you would have lived,
Miklós Radnóti, like your poems – poems the earthworms
did not eat; love as tough as a thistle and as hard to eradicate.

Raking the Powder, 1943

Every day I remove my ring, brooch
and bobby pins, draw the blue serge sack
over my head, tie the laces of my special
shoes — shoes without nails in the soles —
walk up the duckboard ramp and punch
the bundy to begin my shift. The powder
comes to me like a lump of wet clay.
I weigh it, then place it on a heated table
on a handkerchief of Fuji silk, as a bride
might spread her gown out over the bed
before dressing. Once it's warmed, I load
the powder onto a trolley and wheel it
to the charging room. The machine has a plate
with holes like those on a salt cellar.
I slide a tray of caps under the shelf,
open the holes and brush the powder across
the top with a delicate velvet rake.
Push in too much powder and you're history,
but there's a war on, so I don't think
about the danger. Occasionally the boss
takes us, the gelignite wrappers, the cordite
girls and the women who crimp the detonators
into the paddock for a safety drill.
One day he walked half a mile away,
dug something into the earth and marched back.
"This is what happens when you're careless,"
he said, as grass shot into the sky and dirt
rained down on us. We were frightened and
terribly careful afterwards, but you never
think anything will happen to you. We were just
about to finish last Tuesday — you have to clean

the press and the pellets before you knock off —
when I heard this rumble. If it's a pop
you ignore it, but when the floor moves
you know something is wrong. The blast stripped
the protective clothing off her — dress,
shoes, cap, everything but her undies were gone.
Stubble on her forehead like burnt hay.
Skin flaking off the way a dead moth crumbles
in your fingers. The foreman didn't recognise her,
that's how bad she was. I held her and said,
"You'll be alright, love. We'll have you
doing a foxtrot in no time." She loved
to dance. She was barely conscious and had
no use for the truth. At least I managed to lie.

Remembering Hiroshima

i remember waking from one dream
and walking into another
through the blue phosphorescent flames
which flickered like the reels of silent film
like insects trapped in amber the dead
embraced or sat silently at prayer
a woman with a hundred heads was eating air like mad
it was then that i turned away
from the ruins and went to the river
where an animal drifted downstream like an upturned table
so i took the table to ferry people across the river
here the dying looked at the living
and wished that they were dead
while the living felt ashamed to be alive
and wished that they could die
black rain began to fall and the river forgot to flow
so i stepped off the table and walked across the water
in the distance i could see winged horses rising
from the pools of blood on the ground and seas
springing from the earth at the touch of their hooves

David Gilbey

Shrapnel

1.
My father talked about the shrapnel in his chest —
a soldier in the British Army, World War 2 —
his 'little bit of Italy' — a random bomb burst.
Doctors wouldn't remove it —
too close to his heart.
Unlike his memories and his wife, it stayed with him till he died.

This twisted, metal claw of the Great War effort
dug out of the chest of a local farmer
has been burnished to a brooch.
Grendel's talon weighs heavily
looks like a supplicating, misshapen torso emerging from a skull shell
or a refugee riding flotsam on the breast of the museum's table.

Deadly chocolate. Bronze offal.
Solidified turd of the chimeric war-monger.
Diseased, broken yolk of the peace cake ...
precious bane.

2.
Before being blown apart
he sent me pretty postcards from Belgium:
embroidered lilac gothic script matching the thistle head:
'From Your Soldier Boy' — the shards pierced my heart.

Because I saw the other pictures, the obverses:
the sewage of the defrosting trenches, splayed starvation, gassed corpses —
a Medieval holocaust.

Somehow the sentiments of bereavement expressed in verse:
'When I lost you … the roses are now dead'
with their fine, fashionable lovers in English country gardens
never quite made up for the absence of his hands on the milkers …

3.
Leftovers, 1929:
a baked rabbit recipe from the Disabled Men's
Association Cookbook *The Best of Everything*:
five lines for the whole process, from dismembering
to basting and roasting;

a Dance Card ticked and signed
from the Tumbarumba Diggers Turf Club:
three waltzes (plus one for supper),
three one-steps, two foxtrots
and one each of a quadrille and a schottische.

4.
You brought back darkness from the war.
On the farm, in Australian sunlight, you ploughed paddocks of France.
Our bed was a battlefield, a bomb crater.
You'd cry out in the night, grab me hard, shake me,
thinking I was the corpse of your mate.

You were handy — made me a flue-cleaner
from a kangaroo tail, a beater from old wire
a meat cleaver from half a chaff-cutter blade
and a pot-scrubber from chain mail.
But never came completely home.

You didn't mean to hurt me but your eyes looked through my face
to other faces. A woundless wound.
I wondered if my breasts, my body, reminded you of other bodies.
I hoped you were clean or had taken the medicines.

I know other soldiers spent a third of their active service
in the VD wards of European hospitals.

5.

Washday Monday: the copper had to be lit early
water carted from the creek in kerosene tins –
sixteen for an average family wash.
Handmade soap pocked our skin.
Reckitts starch gave us absolution.

I would crochet doylies, weighted with glass beads
to keep the flies from the milk
darn his socks, mend his shirts and pants.
I always thought patching was a labour of love.

I read in the newspaper: 'Problems of the Household'
how smart summer hats and millinery skills
can brighten the cloudiest evenings.

6.

It kept his fire dry, framed the brief candle of his life
this Souvenir of the Greatest War, this matchbox holder
connecting him and his ANZAC mates with English military history.
Its corners and edges are worn back to the metal
its cover scored and stained – pitted by life's cysts
but the hunting horn and king's crown of the Durham Light Infantry
support its ghostly pedigree: 'British Made'.

Whose fingers stroked it, lit up which dark?
In what weathers? Whose pockets?
The spent matches once a Birnham Wood now
totally extinguished – even the ash is scattered.

The back cover flags of Italy, France, Japan, Belgium, Russia
remind Britain of its promiscuous bedfellows
telling different stories of different wars and different alliances.
Australia is an absent concubine.
Authenticity is in the monocle of the beholder.

Andrew Burke

Fireworks Night / China

An annual time to celebrate:
the surrender of the Japanese
at the end of World War II.

Fireworks light the Linfen sky
and Chinese soldiers sing proudly
amplified down Gulou Road East.

It's as bright as a battlefield, loud as a war.
Old soldiers can't hear a thing
and are in bed early.

Ann Davis

O Jerusalem

I have dreamed of you
running in my dreams
as dreamers do
searching
seeking
fleeing from the fear of falling
short of my desire

soldiers armed with death
tread your lanes your byways
but do not see me
in their rush
towards a broken bus
where
sprawling from the shattered windows
no body
waves a welcome

sweating
I race through war-torn streets
and a magdalanian woman
smiles promise from a doorway
then explodes before my eyes

I watch the buildings crumble
within your ancient walls
and again I am
running
looking
yearning for peace

but nowhere here is there
a manger to be found.

S. K. Kelen

Dien Bien Phu

Parachute drop –
I feel the angels' kisses
the ones we'll receive
as we march down victory avenue
our glory inscribed in war's pages
a chapter with the title, Dien Bien Phu.

Words come to mind
to make a paratroopers' song,
the legionnaires' marching tune
returning history and pride to France
redemption – Dien Bien Phu –

schoolchildren wave flags
and sing as we march into view
a flurry of medals & the Germans
we never shot we'll make up for
at Dien Bien Phu.

We'll lure them in and like baguettes
break those rice farmers apart
their backs broken and then their heart
sunk in the mud of Dien Bien Phu –

Uncle Ho and General Zap
will learn a thing or two
first a lesson in soldiery
second is we came back to stay
at Dien Bien Phu.

Our brave and handsome colonel
promised a month's leave
in Noumea and the married guys
can go back to France – in Saigon

I'll array my honey Lotus Blossom
in silk and jewels, stockings from America
and the finest French perfume
when we beat these bastards
making life difficult in Dien Bien Phu.

S. K. Kelen

The Long Trudge

How are you, GI Joe? It seems to me
that most of you are poorly informed
about the going of the war, to say nothing
about a correct explanation of your presence
over here. Nothing is more confused
than to be ordered into a war to die,
or to be maimed for life without the faintest
idea of what's going on.

(Hanoi Hannah 16 June, 1967)

Zippo lighters set village roofs on fire
the country burns like a Roman emperor's
cruel dream. Hell for everyone, but
in the free-fire zones it's a turkey shoot.

A healthy kill ratio of eight to one –
US forces win major engagements.
Superior technology facilitates an effective kill
ratio more like 40 to one though this estimate
includes an unknown number of non-combatants
and friendlies. It's down to better weaponry and massive
firepower – carpet bombing to heat-seeking cluster bombs

some of which don't explode immediately, glittering toys
the village kids pick up and blow off their legs and arms.
A new bomb tested didn't work: a 10,000 pound bomb
the pointy-heads hoped would burn all oxygen at ground level
over fifty acres, suffocate a communist village.
It just thumped on the ground and was captured
by the enemy. Napalm works fine burning forest
& villages so the VC and NVA regulars can't hide.
The daisy cutter is a work of art, more a style of bombing

than the bomb itself. Exploded a few feet above the ground
it clears vegetation and buildings in a perfect circle
with a diameter of 250 feet. People burn sweetly, too.
Dioxin agent orange leaves a lasting gift your children's
children will appreciate. The battle for hearts and minds
was won by the Zippo lighter.

KA Nelson

Say Istanbul

After 'Saga of Istanbul' by Bedri Rahni Eyūboğlu (1913-1975)

Say Istanbul and I don't think of crumbling walls
Byzantine relics, Ottoman palaces, churches, mosques
or museums but two old men in a small alcove
under a stairwell who make tea and coffee all day,
a basket raised by rope and pulley taking it
to the morning residents above.

Say Istanbul and I don't think of the Bosphorus
its seagulls, mighty ships or ferries but fishermen
who line Galata Bridge each day and night
their silver mackerel thrown on hotplates
or cooking in pretty barges bobbing on a choppy
current, decks alight, smoke rising.

Say Istanbul and I don't think of Roxelana, wife
of the first Suleyman who, coming from the slave
trade to his palace, successfully implored him
to kill a rival concubine then his first born son.
I recall good-natured vendors in the Grand Bazaar
spruiking leather, gold, carpets and my blue one.

Say Istanbul and I don't think of going to Gallipoli
but how my father, when alive, had to sit in a certain
chair facing the back door, how he was often very angry
but at peace now, buried in the local cemetery, his air
force plaque paid for by a so-called grateful bureaucracy
and how my brother's PTSD manifests post-Vietnam.

Say Istanbul and I don't think of Christianity or Islam
or any take on God or Allah but my mother's maxim
live and let live. I think of citizens caught up in charges
of *insulting Turkishness,* the arbitrary nature of the state –
theirs and ours – and one carved column in the cistern,
its perpetual tears being shed for humanity.

Jennifer Compton

The One Day of the Year

'The One Day of the Year' is an Australian play by Alan Seymour
written in 1958 about Anzac Day

I saw my husband-to-be in this play in New Zealand
when I was 14.
It was on at the Concert Chamber in the Town Hall
and he played Hughie Cook.

As he reached up to turn off the light on his bedside table
so he could pash Jan
I had the strangest thrill.
I wanted a man (him) to reach for the darkness so he could

discover me. (And so he did.)
If it hadn't been for his world famous programme collection
— "Were you in that play? That was you?" —
years into our marriage

the penny may not have ever dropped.
(The strangest thrill of all.)
As for the play, well
it was about the men who had fought

embodied by men who hadn't.
And I was numbed to the rhetoric
of Anzac Day
how it didn't jibe with the old soldiers

stumbling and inchoate after the Dawn Service
on that one day of the year.

If they could get a grip on
your elbow at the bus stop

– "Don't go today!" Mum would say. "The men are out!" –
they breathed confusion into your face
the lost boy stark staring
all the words dying on their lips.

The row of medals on their lapel
would clank, would bring them back
and they would unhand you like dropping
something too heavy to hold.

Anzac Day

40% of the eligible went. 60% didn't.
To the accompaniment of the Bathurst Railwaymen's Band
23 young men boarded the night train to Sydney.
Robert had heard something
scandalous about the French.
George had family in London.

There is heat in colour, ginger harbours.
As it happened, they invaded and galvanised
a crumbled Ottoman Empire.
Heads full of Gallipoli sand and cocaine
they fought nowhere over nothing
then climbed back on their ships ...
this Old World tour. Hold flesh.
Birds fall off the ride, aloft in recollection.

Apollo follows scratches
while Thor mumbles above
sheep and omens,
chains of yellow gas.

You could be comic, bloody oath —
ignore the horror. This war to prove nothing
bar the fragility of skin. Valour, insubordination, desertion
the expendable colonial number.
More came home seeking silence. Remembrance was a curse.

Some say it heals
to take the old wounds out.
Anzac Day is a construct

whatever the motive. Gunbarrels by candlelight,
empty beer cans fall like spent shell casings.

When I was young the day had lost its candle,
balmed with dust. It was my grandfather's quiet prayer
for the golden brother who died
and his own insignificance mirrored in smaller injury.
Bitterness of his father, the wrong son had returned.

Vietnam changed the settings. My father
who enlisted twice
endorsed (or forgave) the Masters.
Sacrifice. Sidestepping contested family
he shuffled off to the march (1971)
like it was a shameful habit.
Women in bib-overalls marched parallel to *his* parade
commemorating victims of rape in war.
He and I never spoke, I was
vengeful in my pacifism

We are a shard of a generation, those who have not fought/
will not fight.
My eyes too are fixed
dawn is the fatality of night. I try
but cannot KNOW.

When there is nothing left.
We are as Australian as our military ...
at a world buffet
serving chips.
Just after the Easter eggs
comes the regimental colours.
This day gets restored,
like a government lick of paint
and a bucket of movie tears.

To mothball this ceremony
is to put the option
of any future war into that terrible category of "history".
Some said "you have to be out of it
if you want to get into it".
It is holy, but unhealthy. I admit
it will never be mine ...
they once said in remembrance we avoid repetition
but that's been dropped. The parade
will always need new faces, our failure feeds the ranks
as yet again they march across the bones.

Carolyn van Langenberg

My mother's uncle

the tall man
easy in the saddle
squints
juts his jaw at
boundary walls   black
rock striating hillsides
greenly fringed waterways
where the dairy herd lows.

blue sky
vaults and
mocks
straight forward
his gaze
    uncompromised
though turbulence
blunts perception.

I dare to ask, "Did you go?
To Anzac Day? The dawn service?"
His gaze across paddocks
turns where darkly
battle roars, the bullets' whistle
over the cries of lost boys.
"Why celebrate?" he snaps.
"The bloody officers!"

(across oceans
destiny sailed to the bay
dunes towered

he ducked
hard rain
bellowed orders

his grip
frayed, his clear-eyed
faith

slipped
on blood, sweat
shot

into a foxhole
left arm
ripped off)

What does a seven-year-old think?
"They didn't care about us,"
said my mother's uncle,
his adult lip trembling rage,
his arm his dignity his memory
warm skin quivering shreds
stuck in the child's questions.

Susan Hawthorne

Valence (extracts)

all day long the gods have been screaming
their prevalent song of war and pre-emptive strike
war leaves you gobsmacked words slaughtered in the throat

•

that widowed ground has been filled with half-grown trees
almost impassable they are topped by yellow-crowned florets
along each side run sorrow pegs a means to navigate grief
against the fox-pelt cloud a woman stumbles tear-blinded
and half-demented her mind dismantling itself in a meltdown
so profound that buried poetry rises unbidden

the tiger's tongue is red at the root like a meridian
dissecting the fearful symmetry of its body
melting in the delicious buttery light of late afternoon
you dream of Petra's rock red caves imagine the bone dry
severed joints slumped like a ragdoll lumpy and disjoined
cranes settling above that old city in their precarious nests

no ladder long enough to reach them no florin
of pure gold to take you across that stream of air
you know you'd have to pay a bigger price for death
to mint that coinage sometimes you wish you'd learnt more
than just the Hebrew alphabet like raindrops in an eyelash
preciousness is nothingness against silk and stars

in your heart is a great hollow of pain like the chiselled
sound of a cello washing away the world's grief
a pilgrim on that Spanish trek to Santiago
your world turns illegible with its multiplying echoes

all you can do is eclipse the scream stuck in your throat
like a sow at sacrifice roped to interminable silence

•

at the beginning of every year we ask whether
the killing spree is over for now all the soldiers
who heard earth's tinnitus ringing on the frontline
fly home walk through the front gate
cannot explain what they have seen have heard
that there is no longer any grace in the world

in the houses where women keep time with days
over stoves where hunger is the taste of childhood
and thirst a close neighbour no one dares to speak
peace is a mirage a vision at the edge of thought
cities stagnate and are separated from the people
countries are divided like pieces of cake

few speak against revenge slit the veins open
let the blood run a long-fingered violinist
plays a spree of notes emergent gravity looping
as a new virus explodes crossing all the man-made
boundaries taking off on its very own killing spree
rampaging through the gutters into the glare of air

•

in Sabra and Shatila only bodies are left
shadows of screams echoes of eyes
that have stopped seeing stopped recording
a nation's memory will not unwrap when the chain
is nothing but missing links one by one
each memory becomes a wilderness

history is the mind of the patient
crumpled in the hallway after electric shock
fate is an uncut life sentence that fine stalk
of a body bent under the burden of guilt
a left handed idiom that itches beneath the skin
among the cedars of Lebanon gods once lived

•

undoing hatred is a pilgrimage of hurt
power unwinds as much charge as a tangle of wire
we squirm in death's footprint caught in private fogs of affliction
all that energy ebbing in acts of fury the dying swan stilled exhausted
its wings wired its fluttering mind caged and broken
these many-mouthed furies iron-tongued grind their teeth all night long

uncurl your limbs stretch your spine
walk as if the sky's mantle is wrapped about your shoulders
when your breath evaporates look at the world with a split vision
imagine a hawk-eyed view of the oceans
from that height see the vast pastures of plankton
whalefood float with cuttlefish unoccupy your days

•

you dream of flight with wings with claw some days
you sob because all the elegies for the dead all the strings
played with furious pathos will not stop the clot of war

Andrew Lindsay

One and Ha'pence

for Walter, and for Kerry

When the order came to go over the top Wal's mate
was first man up, and was hit instantly, shot and killed,
or that's what the family legend says, and one hopes that
death was instant, and would desperately believe that it was
true, though the human creature is a stubborn beast,
and it took my old man many instants to die, and we had
to wait for the death rattle to turn up to know that the end
was coming, death was taking its time, and had already taken
its toll on us by then, wishing for nothing more than the old
man's speedy death as we said our prayers yet again to the
god of morphine.

Wal's mate fell down dead right then, it's said, and Wal
put his hand above the trench, and one and a half fingers
were blown off, and now that he was wounded he did not
need to go over the top, and so he lived to tell his tale of
trench warfare in Gallipoli. The government paid him a
 weekly pension of one and halfpennies in compensation,
and when the second war broke out Wal gave his one and
a half pennies back, his contribution to the war effort.
Or was it his one and a half fingered salute?

One hundred years later, my stubborn comrade lies dying in
his hospital bed. These last ten years he's spent digging up
the storied bones of dead Diggers, the rebel Irish Anzacs
who fought in Gallipoli, and in France, who then fought
for the Irish after the 1916 Uprising, training the locals and
bearing arms against the English. They were traitors, or
loyal sons, depending only on your disposition.

My dying mate, trussed in a giant nappy, the morphine drip
and the yellow line of his catheter tether him, and on his
61st birthday he tenders a pithy summation: Shit Happens
and one wishes for nothing more than the ability to cut
the lines and set him free, free of his pain, free of the necessity
of living, but at last the end does come, and it's the starkest
blessing, to know that death becomes our liberation.

Rowan, on the shortlist for Iraq

Monotone soldiers stand frozen in the centre
of small tired towns atop blocks bearing
names of our boys, stacked like foundation stones.
Children play with plastic men in the dirt beneath.

Granddad marches to the cenotaph in the dark
with his mates, bugle reveille wailing around
the bones of his chest like the big gun whine
the day his arm was torn and flung into mud.

Squealing tank crawls like an earthquake,
ten thousand drone "devils are on the loose".
Whoever won? There's nowhere new,
so back they go to Crimea Syria Afghanistan:
Tommy Fritz Johnny Abdul Otto Jerry Charlie Ivan Hajji.

Rowan and his bros are laughing in the living room,
cheering their khaki avatars that fall and rise and fall.
The iron hisses beneath my sister's bowed head as she readies
his drab dress.
The single shooter loser hits the ground and dissolves
like improvised dust.

Richard Kelly Tipping

Instant History (Gulf War 1)

They are waiting there with space blankets
in the sandy heat, practicing jumping trenches
and tank traps flamed like Christmas cakes,
sweating good as Bat Boy in their chemical battlesuits.

They are listening to FM stereo at the place of the oil wells,
jogging on the spot in their fatigue Reeboks,
wiping lens cleaner on their automatic cameras
and on their Ray bans.

They are there at the place of the Arabs,
staring at their gods of Hollywood and Disneyland,
filling houses across America with worry.

*

Words hurt first
biting fists.

International Law goes down
bleeding from the mouth, quick punched by
'Shock and Awe'.

Collateral language
keeps popping its head up
out of the bloodied sand

where bodies have become pink mist
swirling in the data smog.

*

The President is repeating:

"Read my lips. This war
is not about prime time television,
free trade monopolies or
cruise missiles packed with trade marks
skimming at street level to the right address.

This is just another
blessed Thanksgiving,
sharpening the knife
for the fat pink turkey."

Rozanna Lilley

Nothing but sunflowers

Surface-to-air the sunflowers bloom
        foolhardy with pollen heads turned brazenly
Toward the banking blue
        nudging vast fields of ripened wheat
Slipstream duets of birdsong and bombs
           a windblown hit parade

At four forty five the rains came
        swollen with life
Clouds fat with bodies
        two hundred and ninety eight transits
The dry earth momentarily melting
        a grid square picked bare

'We did warn you – do not fly in our sky'

In the gathering darkness they lower
        settling garlands of grief
Each folded petal ruched   soft pleating
        the day's swift shredding

Vertigo of familiar flightpaths dismembered
        Still strapped to their seats

On the World Stage

for Paul McGeough

Newspapers
piling up day by day
and the macabre tidings
from the Iraq war
get wedged in my conscience.

A fraudulent war
sugar coated with euphemisms
anointed with desert oil
a deadly 'asymmetric confrontation'
with unbridled momentum.

A super-duper weaponry's war.
Yet precision bombs miss their target
and people vaporise into a "pink mist".

"Stuff happens"
quibbles unashamedly the warmonger
naming the holocaust
as a mere "untidiness" of freedom.

There, in a ruined hospital, lies
beautiful twelve-year-old Ali Ismail
who "has the lithe body of a sportsman"
but no arms. They were burnt to the bone
and charred along with his parents
three siblings and ten relatives by a US missile.

Now many Western newspapers
and some compassionate celebrities
bask in the limelight of his agony
raising funds for his prosthetic arms.

There, the grief-stricken
Razek al-Kazem al-Khafaj
mourns his wife, his six children
his father, his mother
his three brothers and their wives
killed by an American rocket.

There, the fair baby Amir Yas
writhes ablaze in his father's arms.

Ali Ismail,
Razek al-Kazem al-Khafaj,
Amir Yas,
protagonists
in the tragedy of war
make a transient entrance on the world stage
of the mass media.

Backstage suffer the multitudes.

Sydney 2003

TV Doco, 2012

"We're burning daylight"
says the sergeant   "Let's go"

The IED goes up:
        "There's the money shot"

To win a war, to inner war ...

        "Nobody move
        even if a snake bites you
        even if a bee stings you
        until the flag is raised.
        This is our flag."
yells the Afghanistan sergeant
to the square of local troops.

        "The Taliban come from this land"
says a man in the market.

        "It's a mind fuck. It's debilitating.
        Marines don't fight wars, they fight battles."
says a marine, head shaking.

Marines in a mud building pay $2500 a life
lost in the unfortunate SNAFU (all four were girls):
        "We are giving you
        the very least
        that we can do
        in this condolence payment
        since you can't bring back
        someone you love"

Kevin Brophy & Les Wicks

The Redactions

2014 intercepted electronic communications, DOD ...
aphorism identified as a threat to national security.

The aphorism envies the novel,
the novel, of course, envies the haiku
and the haiku envies the brief life of the leaf.
– Gen PJ Burke, U.S. Army War College

Authority is the kernel of riot
– Prof Emma Burg, LSE

War and *Peace?*
– Leo Bradley Tolstoy, Christian Agent in North Korea

1.   The Department of Sand
Cpl Raymond Sands to Anthony Sands (brother)

With my surname, of course the bastards sent me to Iraq,
every leader leads to defeat this war
that "finished" years ago the green zone
glows in the dark *we are the aliens.*
The sky is falling... those habits of our hats
I have a life back home.
Failure is a sun.

2.   The Department of Grease, MCB Camp Lejeune, NC
Pvt Peter Pitz to Terry McAnulty (high school auto teacher)

Thought the Marines were a real big deal – I'm not
some kind of hero. I fix cars. Always thought
you were an idiot. You said
every soul needs a plumber. I know
you can't stay mad when you're never hungry

but *the walls expand to fit one's waistline.*
I've maybe had enough.

3.   Naval Intelligence Camp Lemonnier, Djibouti
Lt Margaret Tannis to Cecilia Breen (wife)

Joy rationed is hungry. I have a job
because I have a language. You said
the light at the end of the tunnel is the way in, not out.
You said *the future is always knocking down the front door of the present.*
But there are oceans, not doors between us.
Tight focus on a loose shoreline, the bay will have its way.
But the way is away.

4.   ICBM silo Great Falls, MT
Pvt 1st class Danny Thompson to Clarice Thurgood (girlfriend)

Your feet leave the ground when you dance
in the shit again, (*embarrassment is the source of all bravado*)
− fell asleep during a 12 hour shift (*over there is your enemy*)
and left the access gates open.
To see you again last weekend
to leave you again last weekend. *Oxymoron: man kind.*
About that fight, don't worry about it
hate is too much like factory work.
I love you Clarice, *we habitually pluck, tie weights to ankles −*
yet are not birds.
I love you like walking
though those words are still plumage, this man's music
the old avian strut about the concordat of hens.

You see, war (love) brings out the poet in me
for the poets are still wildly read
even here in this tedious purgatory.

5.   Langley Air Force Base, VA
Col Jason Driggton to Emily Driggton (daughter)

Don't trust the faith of those who failed to falter.
Your decision to leave university
(every single nothing matters)
worries me deeply,
your note *Stop collecting. Now.* Seems to be just nonsense.
I have been where you are.
Have we managed the past?
Where there is no certainty you have to pretend.
Love isn't the answer, it was never meant to be.
Love
Dad

6.   Greensboro Vet Center, AL
former Cpl David Alborsen suicide note

There is a sanctity in our best defeats
all my friends out there *(Forget your education!)*
that's where you stayed so
get fucked. *The story of your life will be that it ended.*

7.   Washington Navy Yard– Community Relations, DC
Senior Chief Petty Officer Rosa Trejos draft valedictory circulated to
colleagues

25 years *expertise is your enemy.*
I have lied with a careless grace
for truths that barely matter.
Wisdom is a tribe that demands regular sacrifice.
I have forgotten how to look back.
Never judge a word by the company it keeps.

4 Peace?

Dael Allison

Cento for remembrance

There was only one war and it was finishing
any day soon //
if a pack of bones can serve
to make a feast of sun-lit certainty. //

Every twig sound is a target. //
Routine as a child's nightly prayer//
sparrows explode like shrapnel over ploughland //
rolling wing-over down screaming
to a low strafe of running or falling strangers. //
The slump of the newly dead, / the yaw of the pit,
its shapeless, tumbled meal. //

War is the will of the people
rushing from light //
with bullets for their breast //
but not this other \ disturbance
the absence voice hoarse and faint the call for water //
the sound of man swallowing blood. //
What's the use of such pure courage? //

Is there some harshness in the air
that qualifies us being here //
where canon fire and fingers reaching out
to take a telegram intersect? //
Whole populations go shunted down branchlines
toward the nowhere grid of wire and floodlights. //
These, the regular dead, \ will go under utterly,
\ as their names / went, launched on stray splinters. //

We thought we had buried war with the Unknown Soldier
safe in the stone and rotting away with the flowers //
but wars do not finish: it is not over. //

Wake at nights \ gulp the unspeakable threat \ lie still //
the pit of ash beneath our tongues. //\

Katherine Gallagher 'The Last War'// Margaret Scott 'Peace and War'//
Vincent Buckley 'The Arts of War'// Alan Gould 'Skagen Elegy'// Alan
Gould 'Australian War Cemetery, Pozières'// Geoffrey Dutton 'A Wreath
for Anzac'// Pete Hay 'Frances Turner and Maria Luisa Alcade Gonzalez
at la Colonia, Viznar, 1936'// Douglas Stewart 'Sonnets To The Unknown
Soldier'// 'David Campbell 'Men In Green'// Thomas W. Shapcott 'Sestina
with Refrain'//+// Vincent Buckley 'ANZAC Day'// Tim Thorne 'To Ashes'
// Vincent Buckley 'ANZAC Day'// Alan Gould 'Skagen Elegy'//+// Alan
Gould 'Australian War Cemetery, Pozières'// Douglas Stewart 'Sonnets To
The Unknown Soldier'// Thomas W. Shapcott 'War' // Thomas W. Shapcott
'Sestina with Refrain'// Katherine Gallagher 'The Last War'//

Manifestly

i'm racist
only against
rat races

won't fly
a flag
except one

all white
like silence
bordering on

peace

Anzac Ceremony 1983

She
Stands in silence
In her school yard at Randwick
With hundreds of other girls
The Aussie flag whirls
Like the skirt of a dervish
Solemn sincere
She feels a burning in her nose
And wills her eyes not to cry
Sandra blows a bubble (with her grape flavoured hubba bubba)
Other girls giggle
Aussie girls – so pretty but so disrespectful

She wants to ask for another minute
For the Turkish soldiers
But dares not
Lizzy already teased her about killing Mel Gibson in the movie
'Gallipoli'
'A treat' the deputy had said 'for Anzac Day!'
For many years after she will think 'a treat' is something bitter

She could easily punch Lizzy or Sandra
Or any of the girls who give her a hard time
But her parents ...
Won't get it
They don't know about the neither, nor
The rift between home and playground law
A.K.A.
Second generation Turkish Australian shit
She wants to break Liz's nose but not her dad's heart
Her seyi senin icin biraktik CANIM KIZIM

Utandirma beni, adam gibi oku
So she behaves well, like a good Muslim girl

She feels sad for the ANZAC boys
It wasn't their fault
But what the hell where they doing on the other side of the world
Trying to choke a 'sick-man'
Messing with her mum and dad's land
Just to look good for England

Her history teacher Mr. Pavros (who hates Turks for sure) says
It's called TRENCH WARFARE girls, the ANZACs had no chance
In her gut she knows better
But
Her English is not good enough to express what she feels
When I grow up I'll make a movie about Gallipoli
Or I'll be a teacher she comforts herself
And my students will stand in silence for two minutes

Prayer

A pincer movement of rain clouds —
we're outflanked in the gassy light
driving through these mid-North towns
which cling to life
the way the topsoil clings
just above the shale.

Boys of milk white stone
bend over their rifles
to inspect the poppies,
plastic, tubercular red,
in crosses at their feet.
The same face in every town,
as though they were brothers.

The car moves into the Willochra plain,
the Southern Flinders like Gallipoli
but with a far more ancient sea.
My children's faces reflect in dust-streaked windows.

May you never crawl or lie
in the stinking charnel
that is the basement
of all empires.

May you run up stony hills
only to picnic or make love.

May you never carry a pack
heavy with death fear or death-wish.

This said silently
to a rear-view mirror.

When we arrive
it's already night.
The sheds where the volunteers came from
grey, looming polygons,
silent of sheep —
a farm only for tourists.
Behind us, the black range,
then stars, what stars —
Rigel (falling) Sirius (falling)

A cold, autumn moon
shining on the blind eyes
of the boy soldiers,
back there,
guarding the sleeping towns.

Alex Skovron

Report from the Lowland

Shuttling between resignation and despair
we survey the corroded trenches
from a height that shrinks them to a scrawl
snaking across a desiccate geography
no atlas could faithfully impart. Many times
we've overflown these 'fields of renown',
as the antique historians attest them;
many times landed among the dead cities
strewn across all the province. Great rivers
are sterile crevasses; towers once mighty,
triumphant, stand skeletal – the dusk
oozing through their silhouetted apertures –
or lie rubbled within their own footprints,
that strode the horizon once from sky to sky.
We traverse awful declinations, outcrops
of absence, remnants of an epoch that stretch
into distances no clock could measure,
futures no calendar will chronicle, a past
entombed in long-forgotten crypts, where
monuments to Time lay commingled
amid its travesties – where a vagabond leaf
from a ravaged book still half-flutters
beside the slabs of its once grand repository,
catches the glance of the sun, the breath
of a breeze, subsides to its dream of words.

Saba Vasefi

Asylum

This pen splatters the page
With my blood, my words download
Anxiety. My memories crack down,
My childhood lies, its forehead broken,
Before me on the page, and voices leak
From it, voices from fig roots
Near the school yard, from bullets lodged
In the blackboard's throat; voices from
A lacerated blood bag; voices
From a veiled girlhood, bruised by
Boot soles and batons. Even the deaf dolls
Dare not cry among the rubble, under
Bombardment.
My skull bones are breaking, and I
Cannot
Peel the panic from my corneas.
I need to launder the shrieks that seek asylum
Under my sheets, so that even the buzzards
Will have to call a moment's truce, observe
A moment's silence,
In honour of the dead
And the living dead whose footprints make
My pages, whose children sleep in war's
Eternal aftermath, my mind.

Weapons

Ruins
corpses in the sun
men moving cautiously
in the abandoned streets
close to the scarred walls.
Men on top of houses, hills,
coming from dark undergrounds,
men holding on, hugging
these metal erections
firing them
a spray of semen
rushing with velocity
to breed another race of killers.

Jeltje Fanoy

Wars

Wouldn't you like
to send th bill

for th effect of WW2
on all of us, to somebody?

my miserable childhood,
spent, painfully, piecing

together th shards
that were my father,

we thought our father
was wilful, unpredictable,

a little crazy, at times,
out of touch, incapable

of understanding,
just when empathy

was needed th most,
something was amiss,

we had to tell him
th simplest things

over and over,
bridging th ruptures

left by his ECT,
he was responsive,

went along, enthusiastically,
basking in our love for him,

we were lucky. After WW1
many came home, to live out

th rest of their lives
shell-shocked,

in turmoil, reliving
th horrors they lived thru

again and again, out of sight,
and away from their children.

Afshin Soleymani

The Lord of War

I like to eat my breakfast in Hanoi, my lunch in the Horn of Africa
and my dinner in the Persian Gulf beside the flamingos.
All of the earth is my territory. I belong to all nations and all nations
belong to me.

Managing of the global village is my biggest concern. I must work
overtime to stabilize the new world order. I am responsible for the
future. I am responsible for the history. I am the lord of war.

Let me start with children. Children are fantastic creatures and I
adore them. They are the convincing excuse to start a war. Of course
they are also the logical reason for truce.
I am an expert weaver. I rip the silk of children's dreams and weave
nightmares for them instead. Amazing recycling!
I know children like to have challenge and emotion. That's why
sometimes I present a scene of real war in front of their eyes. This
is much better than the stupid video games, which are total lie and
unreal. It is a great idea for children to have first-hand experiences
of war.

Did you know I am the unique magician who can quench a fire with a
bigger fire and only one who is able to wash blood by blood?
My lovely slogan is: "war for peace, peace for next war", do you see?
It's extremely meaningful, philosophical.

Oh poor me! Some fool people wrongly call me the warmonger. But
it's unfair because I am only allergic to permanent peace. My private
doctor has recommended me to remain far from peace. That's all.
Even further, some stupid politicians and journalists accuse me of
planning a conspiracy. From my perspective the conspiracy theory is
only a big hallucination apart from the aliens' conspiracy from other

planets that my army is completely ready to defend!

I am absolutely modest but I have to confess that I am a fantastic chess master. Just my chessboard is a little bit bigger than yours. Indeed, earth is my chessboard.
I move my chessmen among the continents and countries.
Some people are proud to be my knights or pawns. They are my faithful volunteers. You can be also one of my soldiers and all Kamikazes welcome!

Did you know your lord is a writer? Yes, I am a creative scriptwriter. Human rights is my favorite theme and my rich producers often prefer to invest their money in this concept. That's why I write new screenplays non-stop; actually my counsellors help me a lot in this.

Oh, it's my lunchtime now. But before I leave, can you guess what my next screenplay is about? And which country will be my next location? A hint, this time it will not be in the Middle East!

Traveller

Once the branches you hold are broken
The paths to your true self are shown
The protecting arms lose all their warmth
Let the traveller continue to travel

First, you look for a place to hide
With a fiery heart you question every soul
You knock on each door one by one
Let the traveller continue to travel

The one you say's a cure — they're looking for a cure
The hay of their life is blown in the wind
They haven't found a cure for the pain
Let the traveller continue to travel

My foolish heart will find its true self
One day it will reach its ocean
The murmuring of Hidayet goes on and on
Let the traveller continue to travel

Translated by Hidayet Ceylan and Matt Hetherington

Fringe Network Anthology Launching, Herbarium, Botanical Gardens

11th of November 1984

on this day
11th of November
1918
the world
celebrated peace
after the war
to end all wars

on this day,
11th of November
1936
my father
arrived from Greece,
and as he descended from the gangplank
all Australia stood still ... or so he said.

on this day,
11th of November
1975
i took off my white coat
locked the laboratory
did not sign the signout book
at Kraft Foods Ltd.
and sped to join 100,000 protestors
yelling general strike
at the gates of Government House.

on this day
11th of November
1975
the trade union leader
said
go back to work
we will go to the polls
we live in a democracy.

on this day,
11th of November
1984
the self proclaimed fringe
reads poetry in the park
just a rifle shot
from the gates of Government House.

there were other wars
my father lived and died unnoticed
the election was lost
the trade union leader became prime minister
and one day, the poets will be carted off to the M.C.G.

Christopher Konrad

'vision of the heart' (*ru'yat al-qalb*)

Talib: *ru'yat al-qalb*
Swanston Street November and the cups are out
cold wind on the neck
Tram-bell: wake up · wake up
vision of the heart · and I will speak to God
tell him your thousand thousand names
'tis November   'tis the eleventh
we will remember · young soldiers on the street
filled with a thousand footsteps

Tariqat: ten stations to God
leaves in the wind · we who do not know how to remember
this month will not forget
Cold wind on the neck

Jill McKeowen

Away from war

'Let the god not abandon us
Who have come so far in darkness and in pain.
We too had our lives to live'
Derek Mahon, "A Disused Shed in Co. Wexford"

A Saturday morning warm as honey flows
in my backyard, where I'm picking strawberries,
reaching into waves of shadowed leaves
for each exquisite berry face, and seeing
desolate faces from last night's TV news:

Syrian women, children, men walking
the railway tracks of Europe, one step then
another, walking away from war, modern
pilgrims carrying faith and bottled water,
money saved, and food in plastic bags.

My strawberries rustle, light as paper lanterns
in the September sun while people walk
towards a peace they know exists; blocked
by state police they plead *We are human! –*
Just like you! – Have children just like you!

By Saturday afternoon I'm in the kitchen
sorting berries, holding the bruised aside,
rinsing red sun-gloss under the tap,
weighing my good fortune on the scales.
The TV news shows buses moving walkers

to a border in the night; one camera
shoots inside a bus, framing the private
gaze of a woman who looks ahead to the road
coming from darkness. Her resting hand protects
the back of a sleeping child, a dreaming breath.

And every night the pictures will come: the sinking
boats, a drowned child washed up to land,
an old man crying as all his life is dumped
with orange lifejackets on a beach, another
who says *I was an accountant, now have nothing*.

I make the jam on Sunday night while listening
to *Lohengrin*, tumble berries and sugar
in the pot, grateful that Wagner's music
proved to be his better angel, moving
minds to feel; the melting mass becomes

a roiling ruby syrup, bubbling trails
of sticky pink, seething, foaming; the music
swells, transcending states for constellations.
I weep with this and further news: the people
of Munich clasping the hands of Syrian arrivals,

holding signs of *welcome,* ابرحم.
At the end of Act 1, the jam has set. I guide
it into jars, admire completion of small
good things, the jewelled faces of fruit
pressed against the glass. Blessed, I hope

for all a garden, music, lives to live.

Note: ابرحم = *marhaba* (Arabic for *hello*)

208

C * Ç = C

(Cento anni son passati da una era piena di sangue
via un paese di diversi nomi per secoli; adesso, Çanakkale
ed una Casa diventa lo stesso paese ai popoli di tante terre)

From afar peoples gathered about homes farther
From far, far lands to one destined other
So as to apart the another into another far
Yet, unawares, stitching it with their own tighter
With most crimson needles firmer, firmer!

As a knot growing tighter, way than that of a Gordian
Struggled to loosen as at length as the covered ocean
As *if* to sew a cerise ensign with hands sanguine
Yet, it dressing into a den stiff with poppies then
Inspiring stories with full-blood apples to origin.

Now under a sky so blue of endless tears and sweat
With the stars blushed to poppy's shame bred
By the hands tearing the another but own apart;
And winter-bright with pride of a defeat triumphant
There stands a home blossomed greenest in violet.

A home of thousands suns warming up all our souls as ever
Souls of all the others standing with noble sprouts together.

Yüreğinin olduğu yerdir evin,
Asıl ulusun tinindeki rengin.

Mathematics

If a man should die
In the night, move on
If we should stop and
Not get up, on the
March, in the ice

If half of us should
Die tonight, and half
Again tomorrow, I'm sure
The mathematics will
Work themselves out

Charlotte Clutterbuck

Kindling

History doesn't bother with her name,
the mother of Icarus.
Did she stand in Knossos, waving
hoping the adventure would be worth
the waxy wings, his fragility,
and then return to slapping bread
against the wall of her beehive oven?

And Sarah, we can safely assume
didn't share Abraham's conviction
that fidelity to divine power
required him to kill what he held most dear.
Did she wonder, as Isaac's figure
walking beside the laden ass
receded, first tiny, then invisible
in the sacrificial distance,
who would chop the wood
for the unsacrificial fires of home?

And far from the icicles
and isolation of Stalingrad
when the Ivans
　　　　those who were left
　　　　after the panzers and the Luftwaffe,
　　　　after their own Red Army
　　　　hurled them, unarmed, untrained,
　　　　half-fed, amongst the rubble
finally killed the frozen Fritzes,
　　　　those who were left after
　　　　Hitler's enormous thou-less I
　　　　and a ration of 100 grams of bread

starved them into writing home
Please send food.
The hunger is too much.
how could their mothers
ever decipher the icy script
of those last, undelivered, letters?

In peacetime my son sets sail
on the sturdy wings of his capacity
to make bread, or beer, or a door,
ready to make sacrifices for his sons,
and I'm left with all the other Sarahs
somewhere behind, his distant birthplace,
with feelings too complex to put in a letter,
raising my axe to the kindling.

Anne Elvey

Un-singing Mary's song

I do not magnify
and yet my soul is bent

not to the invader his hand
on the throat, not to the skin —

his tearing — but toward
the moment: the songs

still keeping
country, a mercy

to come, the unbound
child, the hood

removed, this violence
that would upend

to renovate. Does
the sharp glint

of sun on Hubble
bind sight

to a fantasy or to
ancestries themselves —

migrations, cells, sand
sepsis, rhyme, the metre

of a globe gone
terror-mad

as if a veil were all
it took to shatter

recollection, to elide
the older intervention

that clings to boots?
Wipe, do not wipe it off.

Soft to her cheek
this cloth this child

his breath a promise
that is not already dwelling

on land which may
or may not own you.

The wind stirs leaves
and limbs as if to say

who, who, who
entangles matter

with generation
surrender with survival.

Some Wars

some wars are silent
there are no bridges
the songs of the missing

have long died   the country
mimes its history   the eucalypt
the water   the mountain

stand alone   there is
no afternoon where
flesh comes together

where the stories
of the ten thousand years
comes where the clapstick

sings out here history
is silent and the wars
are not acknowledged

we are deprived of heroes
fools and lessons our history
settles on the grass

like an old man sitting down
some wars are silent
and there are no bridges

The General Becomes

do what I say
and you will be free

do what I say
exactly
and you will be free

love me
and you will be free

love me and only me
this way
and you will be free

vote this way
and you will be free

spend this way
incur & repay debt
this way
and you will be free

you in the deserts
you will be free

follow my lead freely
and you will be free

hate these
fight these
and you will be free

work this way
at this time
in this place
in this manner
without complaint
and you will be free

kill these
and you will be free

wear this
and you will be free

suffer and believe
and you will be free

think this way
vote this way
criticise this way
and you will be free

spend and dream
this way
and you will be free

rebel and wear your hair
this way
and you will be free

lie down lie down
of your own accord
and you will be free

give up all thought
of justice

and you will
you will
I promise you
be free

Anne Kellas

A line of peace might appear

(after Denise Levertov)

We had imagined peace —
dark-eyed, Pre-Raphaelite.
Years of staring at night sky had blinded us.
The gunfire orange skies.
Now writing letters in a careful hand
blandishments and blessings clothe me,
rags of love I walk in,
drunk with dreams of peace I dream you,
slender hope I trail you.
Will you write about us?
Will you write about peace?

The irresolution of a death walks with me,
the slipping of time past o'clockness
into silence and into the damnation of silence.
I am mute.
My voice peters out.
Who bears witness?
Alone the sky, the night, this peace.
The branding ceases.
Irresolution walks with me
in the narrow prism of time left over, I am
cast out, on the other side, on

a different shore, bereft.
Bereftedness, who are we now
in this broken land
in this breaking of nations?
Whose sand is this I tread?

Whose hand I take,
whose land,
whose cut
I feel,
in half I fell
here dying.

Will you write about us?
Will you write about peace?

Whose legion
whose foreign land
whose flag?
I am confused:
I'll hold myself quite still.
A winding sheet – who's spinning me?
Who brought me here to fight?
Will you write about us?
Will you write about peace?
We had imagined peace.
Dark-eyed years of staring at black sky.

Remember us.
Clothe us in your poem words.
Make us breathe your peace.
Steep us in your beauty, we
the shades of generations
who did not want to die
who fought for peace
we the people
pray:
Will you write about us?
Will you write about peace?

John Brinnand

Gratitude

Am I grateful
that young soldiers died for me,
for my freedom?

That my country sacrifices its young,
volunteers them to get things going:
Omdurman 1898; Kirkuk 2014; and many between.

That warriors keen for a fight, yearning for a rite,
end with shit in their pants –
heroes all, hell bent for Team Australia.

With the first war undeclared
and the black-corpsed frontier
whitey white-washed, whited out,
repression compels repetition:
a bloody endless game.

So another generation's finest
charge into fiction's breach
and, like a harvest of ripe wheat
rotting in foreign fields,
turn compost for fatuous myths.

Does this make me free?
Am I grateful?

Missing

You don't see them anymore
Young men with safety pins

holding up folded sleeves or
trouser legs   clad in old suits

jackets double breasted,
pants with cuffs that scuff

the city pavements where
they prop up shop corners

politely asking if passers-by
could spare a few coppers.

Young men, skin yellowed
and dry as a fallen plane

tree leaf, bones almost
showing through, skin

stretched so tight
that it might tear.

And their eyes that have seen
too much, too young, now,

still young   see nothing
but the things we wish,

too late,
that they had never seen.

With Jacqueline du Pré

Elgar's Cello Concerto in E minor, Opus 85

She draws chords for an ocean at dawn,
        a wavering along the shoreline,
        a tarry cn the sand.
Elgar's lament on the Great War, wordless
      on this cloudless morning by the sea.

Her body the soundboard.
      We hear *the loss,*
      the loss, an ocean of loss.
Her left fingers like bees at their source;
      her right hand curved to a swan's head.

She leans like a lover to her cello, leans away,
      leads us to a field. And the rose swells
      in double delight, fading to white at the centre.
She has his music by heart, knows how to be
      half-way through life.

From her mother's score and sketch by her pillow,
      fresh melodies skilled to sway the child
      and walks to the tones of forest and sea.
Now his final movement. the swagger and bustle,
      all on stage pitching in.

She's fiery, hair tossed back,
      fills us with ache.
      She too has gone, lost
like them too soon
      and yet. we say, never.

Martin Langford

The Kingfisher's Wings

Let us remember them all.

It is all the same war.

Lay our wings over them —

kingfisher gleams
                over those
         who have died
                in the braiding of spaces —

the wars between instincts and words;
between gestures and genes.

The peoples who vanished like clouds, in the untallied years —
whose tribes were defeated, whose boundaries are shadow and wind.

Those who sat down in the lean years —
because too many bore in the good ones.

Those who were herded by iron into corners of drought.

Let us feather their bones with our stories,
ruffle the air they once breathed with the blue vanes of grief ...

Who were food for the gods.

Or who died in the turf wars.

Because they were bloodline. Or offal.

Because they were part of a text that required them to lose.

It is all the same battle.

The same bitter hormones:
the same tumbleweed — and kaleidoscope — flurry of grounds.

Those who became inconvenient —
who were dealt on the wrong side of claims.

Who were swept from their fields by Napoleon's ants;
by Jenghis' ants, or by Akbar's.

Who knelt for the lens.

Or who lay down and slept, for the drones.

The boys who were not the right type.

And the women who were.

It is all the one war:

to invent ourselves human;
to word ourselves more than we are.

Let us fold them in the azure of our wings.

Those who were defeated by their readings.

Those who played their words against themselves.

Who died for their freedoms.

Who died because terrors like freedom

were too much to bear.

Let us brush them
with the sheen of our attention —

this riffle of lustre, our sorrow —

this brief spill of water and light
which is where we begin.

Kathleen Bleakley

sounds of stones

small stones underfoot
zen gardens
japanese years
my defiant
four year old
self scattering
raked stones

red gravel steps
memorial paths
grey lakeshore
great grandfather's
rowing to turkey
at dawn

stones & wildflowers
on hillside graves
tiny mounds with
wooden crosses

small stones underfoot
once molten
burning downhill
settling in crevices
morphing in
the dark

Nihat Ziyalan

Who remembers?

I don't know most of the passersby
from afar
we smile
greet each other

sometimes distant
always sunny
"the weather will be gorgeous today!"
in the tone of an unopened umbrella
"it might rain!"
we chat

kids next door I have known
since they are babies
got married
I waved
when the bride and groom waved at me

I used up a few chairs
"you've lasted so long, you old geezer!" looks
while watching

there were some who dropped onto a cane from lively steps
as smiles, greetings become trembly
I remember
the lost ones, too
time and again
like the day we first met

I don't know if anyone will remember
me

when I am lost and gone
don't say
"the paths you took will remember!"
that happens in poems only
don't forget that I was a poet

Translated from Türkish by Mustafa Ziyalan

Danny Gardner

It Always Gets Me

When I think I know all about War
When I am cynical of fresh starts
When I tire of tales of courage
When I count the cost in lives
When I feel no more to find —
The trumpeter playing: 'The Last Post';
Signal of regret and yet
It winds its way
Confronting the dark,
It frames the light
To minds lost in the black.
It always gets me.
And I must look up
From the crypt of circumstance
The clouds have lifted ...
The Last Post — the first eyes
Look on my fate afresh
And so do I.
And so must I.

Philip Hammial

In the Year of Our Lord Slaughter's Children

Our Cleft, our Dolittle, our Hiroshima
bombers fame in the Year
of Our Lord Slaughter's Children.

Impossible to read: body tags
at window speeds in the Year
of Our Lord Slaughter's Children.

Not as easy as it looks —
faking bonsai in the Year
of Our Lord Slaughter's Children.

This gulag peepshow's
just a curtain riser in the Year
of Our Lord Slaughter's Children.

Pneumatic patois offering
hetero service only in the Year
of Our Lord Slaughter's Children.

Spanked scouts flanked by
jubilant dads in the Year
of Our Lord Slaughter's Children.

Clearly breached — bush discipline
by animal designers in the Year
of Our Lord Slaughter's Children.

Media death as per the shunt
of supply in the Year
of Our Lord Slaughter's Children.

The History of Whispers superseded
by the History of Shout in the Year
of Our Lord Slaughter's Children.

Gravy-savvy makes
its point in the Year
of Our Lord Slaughter's Children.

A shelf life, this life,
of one year in the Year
of Our Lord Slaughter's Children.

Who now in arrogance stand
will soon in humility squat in the Year
of Our Lord Slaughter's Children.

Gothic enigmas as the ilk
of business in the Year
of Our Lord Slaughter's Children.

Who would approach
must by mincing in the Year
of Our Lord Slaughter's Children.

Renounce psyche, develop
sausage in the Year
of Our Lord Slaughter's Children.

The iconostasis isolates
its crux in manna in the Year
of our Lord Slaughter's Children.

Caught napping, Nurse
becomes expendable in the Year
of Our Lord Slaughter's children.

As bride to be of the Sultan of Itch
she'll matriculate to Scratch in the Year
of Our Lord Slaughter's Children.

Off at a gallop, spurs
dug in in the Year
of Our Lord Slaughter's Children.

Seven sons with her scent
on their fingers in the Year
of Our Lord Slaughter's Children.

Above the cello his crown
askew in the Year
of Our Lord Slaughter's Children.

A small man with a small disease
giving as good as he gets in the Year
of Our Lord Slaughter's Children,

Such is his calling that over a bowl
like a monk he's bent in the Year
of Our Lord Slaughter's Children.

It's a grievous loan
that's cast his lot with lambs in the Year
of Our Lord Slaughter's Children.

It's cash in the hand that fattens
the calf in the Year
of Our Lord Slaughter's Children.

Every supper but
the last compulsory in the Year
of Our Lord Slaughter's Children.

Coins on the eyes
of what we're about to receive in the Year
of Our Lord Slaughter's Children.

Kathryn Hummel

Trench Art

Crafted by hand, prised out of dull hours
now exhibited in cardboard, sharing splendour with
the tarnished spoons and misty bottles of the market table.

Trench Art to spread butter with or to slice open letters
forged by Artists Unknown whose fingers stamped
the salvaged bullets, the flattened fired jam tins
with marks like water or sand on stone.

Fluorescents flare on the dull grain of brass, over
notches cut into the edge of this well-worn scimitar
that idleness curved like the rough path home.

The Trench Art fails to attract. From time to time,
the curator glances over his newspaper:
Authentic, he says, with a sweep of showmanship.
The crowd, knowing bargains, moves on.

Jan Dean

This Old House

"My thoughts are of you"

On the mantelpiece
resting against a brass camel, souvenir
of the war, the silk postcard
gathered grime, until a bright spark
moved it to the family bible
to lie beside five pressed jonquils.

Initially, his mother spoke little
of the day George left; the longest hug
the gate clicked shut, how tall he seemed
in the sulky seat, the stifled tears
how frail she felt, the sighs of pride.

She watched the dog chase after him
with frequent rests
            and its puffed return
to mope for months.

Aylin finds the postcard
faded to a whisper
cleans it with French Chalk
and, like a Braille-reader, touches
the embossed flowers at its edge
as if her fingers could release
            all answers.

Her name means *female*
with moon halo from her maternal line
which gifted her dark and shiny.

How many 'Great' prefixes
would take her back to George, the loving son
who signed the card? He was at Gallipoli
but her family calls it Çanakkale.

The delicate sheen needs display
but will be lost in this bright room.
She admires the Turkish carpet
mosaic lights, exuberant bowls and clusters
of evil-eyes. Opposites mix.
Pale, but redeemed, fits perfectly.

Seher Aydinlik

You Stole My Childhood

You stole my childhood from me
I cannot open the curtains again
I look in fear from the parting window
There is smell of smoke
I don't know if it is day or night
My mum and dad, they cannot hear my voice
Where are my brothers and sisters?
Where is everybody?
I look around in fear
I'm afraid of these sounds I don't understand
I don't want food or water
I want my mum and dad
I want to see my brothers and sisters
Where are they?
Where am I?
This does not look like my home
I want my nice home and my nice garden
You stole my childhood from me
You said War-War
And you took my childhood from me
You all STOLE my childhood from me
You took my toys from me
You left me orphaned
I have nobody now
You stole my sun
The curtains and the windows
I cannot open anymore
I cannot see my friends
I cannot go out to the street
I cannot even eat a sweet anymore
You said War – War

And you stole my childhood from me
I cannot walk and I cannot run
I cannot see anything anymore
I just wait by the door
I forgot tea and the water doesn't taste the same
Aunty neighbour doesn't even come out anymore
I'm afraid there is nobody around
You said War — War
You took my childhood from me
I don't have a toy car, or a doll
I don't have stories or a school
I don't even have a ball
You said War — War
And you stole my Childhood

Seher Aydinlik

Before and After War

Before war
There was a bit of green everything
The clouds were blue and the air was fresh
The water tasted good
Children would play in the park
People would do normal things
Some would work, some would study
and some would do housework
There would be fresh fruits
Fresh vegetables   Fresh bread
People enjoyed their day
Of course some people were sick
Some people were getting treatment
People had hopes for tomorrow
They had expectations and ideas for their future
But the war broke everything
Cannot see green around anymore
The sky is not blue as it used to be
Air is not fresh
The smell of gun powder takes over
Children are afraid to play in the park
People cannot work like before
People are unhappy they forget how to smile
The air is not fresh anymore
Fruit is more expensive than before
It is not easy to find anything
Most factories are destroyed
Cars, busses, trains are gone
People are upset and shaken
Their homes are broken, there is no fresh water
There is no kitchen, no bed, no TV no radio
People ask each other "is the War over" – No answer

Richard James Allen

Great Wars

We kill what we do not understand
but there is no victory in that.
We pack our guns but leave behind our questions.

The memorials remain,
standing to attention in every town.
Carefully carved words,

as impossible to fathom
as the idiom of a long-forgotten country,
haunted by invisible question marks.

A Bombardier on the Bus

you squirm with not enough legroom
on a crowded 442 bus
crossing the Anzac Bridge
pass two bronze soldier sentinels

called *the conscience of Parliament*
broken nose champion prizefighter
large practical hands rest on his knees
jovial smile under a brown bush hat
Tom Uren is travelling home to Balmain

a prisoner of war under the imperial Japanese
sent to work on the Burma-Thai railway
now a tourist destination:
> *Major attractions*
> > *include the River Kwai*
> > > *3 war museums   2 war cemeteries*
> > > > *and the one and only   Death Railway!*

an uncle of mine died at Changi
refrained from asking *did you know him?*
remember photos of skeletal survivors
Weary Dunlop   forced marches   the disease

Anzac day celebrating war
that's really what he fought for?
kids wear medals of great-grandfather's sacrifice

pass billboards *want longer lasting sex?*
burnt out rubble
> dodgy fire at the White Bay Hotel

abandoned Power Station sprawl
the predator (infamous hot sex blogger) *doing it*
there among the pipes   concrete and aerosol scribble
heritage-listed   asbestos contaminated   toxic war zone!

Tom Uren was witness in Japan
distant mushroom cloud   atom bomb
          dropped on Nagasaki
he protests war in Iraq and Afghanistan
          marching out the front
I hobbled along   back in the throng
Tom Uren tells me *you stay in your seat*
until the bus stops
                    you could fall

John Carey

On Reading Geoffrey Robertson

A tribe of ants negotiates with another species
under the watchful eyes and poised military boots
of polyglot mercenaries who have hijacked the war
for as long as their fragile alliance holds up
and bewigged wise heads still call the shots.
The Rule of Law peeps through a break in the clouds
from time to time when the weary Storm-Gods
sleep at their posts or answer a call of nature.
Might and Right can dance a provisional mazurka
soon broken off but never quite forgotten.

Katrina Larsen

The Cenotaph

Unknown soldier of
translucent copper scrubbed to
reveal your rich blood.

The Great Pain We Feel.

Guided by the nights
Southern Cross, etched white in an
inky granite slab.

Come Back, Return Home.

Red stone towers grow,
imported to rest among
cabbage trees and flax.

Kuia waits, a
hole where her face should be.
An empty face.

The bronze cloak hangs. a
weaving of expectation,
on tired shoulders.

Te mamae nui I a tatou.

Haere mai, hoki mai ki te kainga.

The karakia
resonates, though no lips move
in the space that is

an empty face.

Muddy pigeon tears
adorn the stone at her feet.

Carolyn Abbs

Slow Walk Home

Lucas, age three, studies
detail on the pavement: stone
sweet-wrapper, weeds, and now
a wild poppy sprouts through a fence
He stoops to smell it, as if
it might be perfumed like a rose

We stare into its black centre

***

A fifties London street, November, foggy
I delve into a tray of scarlet poppies,
not play   choose one   drop pennies in a tin,
not stare   at the man in the black leather helmet,
the war   shrapnel ...

Wellie boots chafe welts in the backs of my knees

***

We stroll in the warmth of southern sun,
I will boil an egg for his lunch,
teach him to tap-tap, open the top with a teaspoon,
butter bread, cut it into 'soldiers'
to dip in the yolk

That he never need know about war

Renee Pettitt-Schipp

The Politics of Entry

Coming in the back door
like you could wait politely at the front one.
Coming in the back door
like survival was a party, you're just not invited.
Yet in all this facelessness
there is the coming from;
coming from a landscape in shadow
where rape is tactical, procedural, political
h*old the daughter still*
plant your flag in that dark place,
force the life out of her eyes until she
is pregnant with the violence of it.
Let despair grow round
and firm and hungry.
We say; the welcome mat,
red carpet, flood gates open
when all you see is light
from darkness
a door ajar

Renee Pettitt-Schipp

The Will of Water

Cocos (Keeling) Islands

Out beyond ideas of wrongdoing and rightdoing,
there is a field. I'll meet you there.

When the soul lies down in that grass,
the world is too full to talk about.

— Rumi

Out beyond the reef
beyond the horizon, beyond
the breakers
there is a space
that will break
that will break, that will
unmake you

out beyond the breakers
beyond borders, tankers, customs
freighters
out beyond eyes
beyond sight and the light
of conscience

hear the timbre of strain
sing a low, sad song
this vessel was never meant
to contain such weight

out in the middle of
we will decide who comes

and in the thick of *the circumstances*
every fear of each imagined ending
will engulf you
for we are a land that will not
a law that will not
give

out where mothers
are grasping for children's limbs
we are losing patience with pity, turn away
we will not witness, it will not stick
for we did not see
heard no screams
let me wash my hands in the
they are not my deeds in the
I know nothing of the
will of water

out beyond the ocean
and all its undoing
you had a dream. I will meet you there
for when life is at last allowed its living
the world will be too full
to write about.

granary

there hungry children squat
in the concrete dust   stare
into numb verbs of a lens
caked in grey grains of attrition
dry eyed gods offer zilch
contrition

here people brag about
buying a new car getting rid
of that old bomb have had it
since the sydney olympics   there
the car is the bomb and the bomb
is the car   plenty of roar then plenty
of scrap   in each place a metallic arena

celebrity chefs spray tables with palmfuls
of flour preparing fresh bakes for couchloads
of dilettante viewers   take care how you fold
the mixture   everyone eager to wolf it
down   this is the odour of history

Jill Jones

Remains the Same

All those lost names
    burnt or broken
in the seizures of
    late days.

Where love is the fire
    of forgetting.
Where we are made to dig
    our own graves.

What is the sign of
    collaboration?
Dirt under boots
    match in the hand?

The old excuses
    tamed.

Notes On Contributors & Acknowledgements

Carolyn Abbs is a Western Australian poet published in leading journals and anthologies such as *Westerly*, *Cordite*, *Rabbit*, *Axon: Creative Explorations*, *The Best Australian Poems 2014*, *Australian Book Review*, *Australian Poetry Journal*. Her debut collection, *The Tiny Museums*, is published with UWA Publishing (2017).
Slow Walk Home was previously published in *The Tiny Museums* (UWAP, 2017)

Linda Adair is a Sydney-born editor, writer, designer and manager who graduated with Honours in English from Sydney University and has an MA in Sustainable Development from Macquarie. At a Poet's Union reading back in 1985, Anna Couani introduced her to Mark Roberts. That life-long partnership has produced two amazing offspring as well as *P76* magazine & Rochford Street Press books — all whilst juggling full-time work and striving to write poetry. Her maternal grandfather served at Gallipoli, and other major battles including Ypres.

Susan Adams, PhD, publications include: Gargouille, Regime, Southerly, Westerly, Cordite, Quadrant, 4W. Awards include 'Commended' 2012 O'Donoghue Int. Poetry Competition (Ire), 'Highly Commended', Val Vallis Award 2012 'Highly Commended', Adrien Abbott Poetry Prize 2012, ('Commended', Tom Collins Poetry Prize, 2015, short listed, the Axel Clarke Poetry Prize, 2014, 'Highly Commended' Yeats Poetry Prize 2015. Her first book *Beside Rivers*, (Island, 2013) 'Commended' in the Anne Elder National Literary Awards.

Poem previously appeared in *Southerly*.

Adam Aitken's last books were a memoir *One Hundred Letters Home* and a poetry collection shortlisted for the Kenneth Slessor Award *Archipelago*, both from Vagabond Press. He is the great grandson of a Gallipoli veteran, and son of a prominent Vietnam Moratorium anti-war campaigner. He teaches at the University of Technology Sydney.

Richard James Allen is an Australian born poet whose writing has appeared widely in journals, anthologies, and online over forty years. His latest book, *The short story of you and I*, is forthcoming from UWA Publishing. He has a critically acclaimed career as a multi-award-winning writer, director, choreographer and performer for stage and screen (www.physicaltv.com.au).

Dael Allison writes poetry, essays and fiction and is a Doctoral candidate in creative writing, University of Newcastle. Poems from her book *Fairweather's Raft* (Walleah Press) featured on Poetica, ABC radio. She has edited and published numerous anthologies, most recently *Brew, 30 years of Poetry at the Pub, Newcastle* (2018). Her grandfather Lt Col Arnold Brown fought in Gallipoli and France in Wordl War One, and again in World War Two, in the Middle East (where his platoon created an original Rats of Tobruk medal for him, and where his son also served and died) and New Guinea.

Seher Aydinlik Born in 1953 in Turkey and arrived in Australia in 1991. Visual art practice and writing poems were a big part of her life from a young age. During her earlier years as a child care teacher, encouraged and shared her love of art with many children to enrich their creativity. Since 2005 she has been an active member of the Auburn Artist's Network, sharing her expression of art in many exhibitions as well as volunteering in various roles for the Network. Seher is closely linked to the Auburn community both through her Turkish heritage and as an active artist expressing her creativity and passion in areas such as culture, religion, nature and environment. She has recently won a professional development award for her art work named 'World Within and World Without'. She is also a much-loved author of Turkish poems and has published several poetry books and CD's in Turkey.

Magdalena Ball is a novelist, poet, reviewer and interviewer, and is

Managing Editor of *Compulsive Reader* (compulsivereader.com). She has been widely published in literary journals, anthologies, and online, and is the author of several published books of poetry and fiction, including the recently released poetry book *Unmaking Atoms* (Ginninderra Press).

John Bennett was Sydney Convenor of the international movement Poets Against War and champion the importance of poetry. He served two terms as President of the Poets Union, instigating Poetry on Wheels (POW) tours of regional NSW and his PhD provides an updated Defence of Poetry.

Louise Berry has poems in *Women's Work*, *Food for Thought*, *Grevillea & Wonga Vine*, *We Are Australians*, *A Slow Combusting Hymn*, *Women of Words – Eat*, *Stray'd*, *Love*, *Eucalypt* and community anthologies including Catchfire Press, Central Coast Poets, Poetry at the Pub, Blue Room Poets, Third Wednesday Poets, and Hunter Writers' Centre.

Jenny Blackford's poems have appeared in *APJ*, *Westerly* and *Going Down Swinging*, and have won Australian and international awards. Pitt Street Poetry published an illustrated pamphlet of her cat poems, *The Duties of a Cat*, in 2013, and her first full-length poetry collection, *The Loyalty of Chickens*, in 2017.

"The Interchange" was previously published in *The Loyalty of Chickens* (Pitt Street Poetry, 2017).

Kathleen Bleakley lives with her partner – in life and art – 'pling between the escarpment and the sea, in Wollongong. She has three collections (with Ginninderra Press): *Azure*, 2017; *Lightseekers*, photography by 'pling, 2015; and *jumping out of cars*, with Andrea Gawthorne, images by 'pling, 2004.

Sounds of Stones previously published in *Lightseekers* (Ginninderra). Margaret Bradstock has six published collections of poetry, including

The Pomelo Tree (winner of the Wesley Michel Wright Prize) and *Barnacle Rock* (winner of the Woollahra Festival Award, 2014). Editor of *Antipodes* (2011) and *Caring for Country* (2017), Margaret won the Banjo Paterson Poetry Award in 2014, 2015 and 2017.

John Brinnand is privileged to live, write, rant and dream on Gubbi Gubbi land.

Kevin Brophy's newest book is *This is What Gives Us Time* http://gloriasmh.com/books/this-is-what-gives-us-time/

The Redactions previously published in *Cordite*.

Andrew Burke has been publishing since the Sixties. Over the years he has published 13 books of poetry, 1 novel, a number of short stories, little plays, and a couple of songs. He had a career in advertising then changed in mid-life to academia. He now lives a quiet retired life in Western Australia.

joanne burns is a Sydney poet. Her most recent poetry collection is *brush* Giramondo Publishing 2014. She has recently completed a manuscript of new poems – *apparently*.

John Carey is an ex-teacher of French and Latin and a former actor. He has published five collections of poetry, the latest *Duck Soup & Swansongs* (Ginninderra Press 2018).

Anne M Carson's poetry has been published internationally and widely in Australia. *Writing on the Wall* was published in 2017. She has been recognised in many poetry prizes and is also a visual artist and essayist. She serves as Director Arts on the Ondru Board. www.annemcarson.com

Hidayet Ceylan worked as an engineer in his homeland Turkey before emigrating to Australia in 1997. He has continued to work as an Engineer and Experimental Scientist in Melbourne since then. He has been writing poetry since 1999 but mainly in the last three years, inspired particularly by Erich Fromm, Frantz Fanon, Yunus Emre and Sufi philosophy. He perceives poetry as a self-discovery and he tries to reflect his deep emotions in his poetry.

Charlotte Clutterbuck won the David Campbell Prize in 2009 and has published four collections of poems: *Soundings* (Five Islands, 1997) *Ion* (Piccolo, 2012) *Brink* (Picaro, 2013) and *Shift Control* (Picaro, 2017)

Robbie Coburn was born in Melbourne and grew up on his family's farm in the semi-rural locality of Woodstock, Victoria. His poetry has appeared or is forthcoming in *Poetry*, *Meanjin*, *Island*, *Westerly*, *Overland*, *Cordite* and *Going Down Swinging*. His new collection *The Other Flesh* is forthcoming.

Jennifer Compton lives in Melbourne and is a poet and playwright who also writes prose. Her poem, *Now You Shall Know*, won the Newcastle Poetry Prize in 2013, and is the title poem of the book Five Islands Press published in 2014.

Halee Isil Cosar is a Sydney based teacher, poet, spoken word and community artist. She has been published in journals and anthologies; Australian Poetry Journal, Mascara Literary Review Poetry Without Borders and others. She is passionate about collaborative projects that take poetry outside the page and onto the public platform. Her first collection of poetry *hijabi in jeans* was published by Guillotine Press in January 2018. haleecosar.com

Anna Couani is a Sydney writer and visual artist who runs an art gallery in Sydney. She has published 7 books, the most recent being poetry chapbooks, *Small Wonders*, Flying Islands Press and *Thinking Process*, Owl Press. The grandfather mentioned in Grandpa Alive, was Stefan Siedlecky.

Ann Davis now resides in Canberra. Ann isn't quite sure how it happened, but she seems to have morphed from Wordsmith to Granny and is loving every minute of her new life. *To End All Wars* will be her first appearance in print in some time.

Jan Dean, a former visual arts teacher, lives at Lake Macquarie. Success in competition enabled her to read her poetry in diverse venues including the Powerhouse, Brisbane; New South Wales State Parliament and the International Peace Day Ceremony, Cowra. She was the first female president of Poetry at the Pub, Newcastle, where she is a life member.

Ross Donlon lives in Castlemaine. His books include *The Blue Dressing Gown*, *Sjovegen (The Sea Road) 50 tanka for Alvik* and *Lucidity* (2017). Winner of the Dorothy Hewitt Fellowship and two international poetry prizes, he is widely published in Australia and Ireland. 'The Piano Tuner' recalls the short life of his great uncle, Edward Lang.

Daniel H. Dugas is a poet, musician, and videographer. He has participated in solo and group exhibitions as well as festivals and literary events in North America, Europe, Mexico and Australia. His tenth book of poetry, co-written with Valerie LeBlanc, *Everglades* has just been published by Les Éditions Prise de parole. daniel.basicbruegel.com

Stefan Dubczuk is a Perth architect (Fellow AIA). Awards: Glen Phillips Poetry Prize 2013; second 2015 Yeats Poetry Prize Australia. Shortlisted: ACU 2015 Poetry Prize; SecondBite Poetry Competition 2014. Longlisted: Best Australian Poems 2014. Published: several journals. Anthologies: *Wonderment; Peace, Tolerance & Understanding; Memory Weaving.*

Anne Elvey, author of *White on White* (2018), *Kin* (2014) and *This Flesh That You Know* (2015), and co-author of *Intatto-Intact* (2017), is managing editor *of Plumwood Mountain: An Australian Journal of Ecopoetry and Ecopoetics.* She holds honorary appointments at Monash University and University of Divinity.

'Un-singing Mary's song first appeared as part of an essay: Anne Elvey, 'Reading the Magnificat in Australia in Contexts of Conflict', in *Ecological Aspects of War: Engagements with Biblical Texts*, edited by Keith Dyer and Anne Elvey, with Deborah Guess, 45-68. Bloomsbury T&T Clark, 2017. Reprinted with permission.

Raymond Evans is author of the recent poetry collection, *Half Century, Fifty Poems, Personal and Political* (Adelaide: Ginninderra Press, 2017) He is also a well-known Australian social historian, writing about the Australian frontier, gender relations, war and society study, convict history, popular culture and conflict studies. His work also includes memoir of a less challenging kind.

Rangi Faith was born in the South Island of New Zealand and educated at Canterbury University, Christchurch. His poetry books include *Unfinished Crossword* (1990), *Dangerous Landscapes* (1994), *Rivers Without Eels* (2001), *Conversation With A Moahunter* (2005) and *Spoonbill 101* (2014).

Jeltje Fanoy has been writing, editing, publishing and recording poetry since the 1970s, and is a founding member of collective effort press and Melbourne Poets Union. Her latest collection *Flying into the hands of strangers*, references the post war migrant experience and what it is to live in Melbourne today.

Clare Feldman (1927-2014), poem submitted by Kathryn Fry.

Kathryn Fry has poems in various anthologies, including *Australian Love Poems*, *A Slow Combusting Hymn*, *Watermark*, *Home is the Hunter* and the Newcastle Poetry Prize anthologies of 2014 and 2016. Her first collection of poems *Green Point Bearings* was published in 2018.

Angela Gardner is the author of four collections: *Parts of Speech* (UQP, 2007) winner *Shapcott Poetry Prize*; *Views of the Hudson* (2009) and

The Told World (2014) both from Shearsman UK; and *Thing & Unthing* (Vagabond, 2014). In 2018 she was awarded an Australia Council project grant. She edits at www.foame.org.

Ilium (after Sidney Nolan's Gallipoli Series) first appeared in *Australian Poetry Journal:*) APJ 3.1. *The Cool Shade* was written as part of an AHA *Artist in Residence 'Conflict in History'* UQ Art Museum/ HPRC. Both poems were published in *The Told World* (Shearsman Books, 2014).

Danny Gardner is a freelance editor, journalist, novelist and poet from Sydney. He has convened Live Poets at Don Bank, North Sydney since 2003. He has also co-ordinated Auburn Poets & Writers Group since 2014. His last book was *Brains in My Feet* (Ginninderra) in 2014.

David Gilbey's most recent poetry collection is *Pachinko Sunset* (Island, 2016). He is current President of Booranga Writers' Centre and editor of *fourW: new writing* and Adjunct Senior Lecturer in English at Charles Sturt University. Three times he has been a Visiting Professor of English at Miyagi Gakuin Women's University, in Sendai, Japan. David has been a regular broadcaster on ABC Riverina and sometime reviewer for *Australian Book Review* and *Cordite*.

'Shrapnel' was previously published in *Pachinko Sunset*, Island Press, 2016.

Eve Gray lives in the Lower Hunter; worked at the ABC, graduated with an English triple major from UNE. Her poetry, fiction and features have been widely published and broadcast here and overseas. Nature and its animals (native or human) provide much inspiration, all of which she finds totally absorbing.

Jeff Guess. Born in Adelaide, Jeff Guess teaches English in country and metropolitan secondary schools, 'Writing Poetry' at the Adelaide Institute of TAFE, and tutors at the University of South Australia. His first book *Leaving Maps* appeared in 1984 and was hailed by Judith Rodriguez in The Sydney Morning Herald as 'a major collection'. Since then ten collections have been published, the most recent being *Autumn in Cantabile* (2012). Jeff has written three textbooks on teaching poetry and edited nine poetry anthologies. He has won numerous prizes for his poetry and been awarded six writing grants.

Philip Hammial has had thirty-two poetry collections published since he arrived in Australia in 1972. His most recent collection – *Detroit and Selected Poems* – was published by Sheep Meadow Press in NY in September 2018.

Susan Hawthorne is the author of nine collections of poetry including *Lupa and Lamb* (2014), *Limen* (2013), *Cow* (2011) and the chapbook *Valence: Considering War through Poetry and Theory* (2011). Her most recent book is *Dark Matters* (2017) a novel concerned with the erasure of and war against lesbians.

Pete Hay is a poet from Tasmania and writes almost exclusively thereupon. His latest work, *Physick*, was shortlisted for the 2018 Tasmanian Book Prize. A volume of essays will be published in 2018.

Gail Hennessy has been published in newspapers, literary supplements, journals and anthologies. Her poetry has won local and national prizes. In 2009 her collection, *Witnessing*, brought many of these published poems together with new poetry. Her second collection *Written on Water* was published in 2017 by Flying Island Books.

Matt Hetherington is a writer, music-maker, and moderate self-promoter living in northern New South Wales. He has been writing poetry for over 30 years, and has published 4 poetry collections and over 300 poems. His first all-haiku/senryu collection *For Instance* was published in March 2015 by Mulla Mulla Press. He is a dude. He may even abide.

Hilary Hewitt is an inner-Sydney based writer of poetry and fiction. Her work has been short and long listed in national micro fiction and short story competitions and published in a range of journals and anthologies.

Kathryn Hummel has written four books of poems: *Lamentville*, her fifth, is forthcoming from Math Paper Press. Editor of *Verity La*'s 'Travel. Write. Translation', Kathryn holds a PhD in narrative ethnography and lives intermittently in South Asia. Her award-winning digital media/ poetry, creative and scholarly prose has been published and presented worldwide.

Andy Jackson has featured at literary events and arts festivals in Australia, India, USA and Ireland, and lives in Castlemaine. His most recent collection, *Music our bodies can't hold* (Hunter Publishers 2017), consists of portrait poems of other people with Marfan Syndrome.

Judy Johnson has six poetry books and several chap books. She's won many prizes for individual poems, and for collections: the Wesley Michel Wright prize (twice), Victorian Premier's Prize and shortlisting in the WA Premier's Prize. Her verse novel 'Jack' was on the syllabus of both Melbourne and Sydney University.

Jill Jones has published ten books of poetry and a number of chapbooks. The most recent are *Brink*, *The Beautiful Anxiety*, which won the 2015 Victorian Premier's Prize for Poetry, and *Breaking the Days*, shortlisted for the 2017 NSW Premier's Literary Awards. *Viva the Real* is due in late 2018.

'Remains the Same' first published in *Broken/Open* (Salt, 2005).

Antigone Kefala is a poet and prose writer. She lives and writes in Sydney. She has published several collections of poetry and prose including *Absence* (Hale & Iremonger, 1992) and *Sydney Journals* (Giramondo, 2008). Latest poetry collection *Fragments* (Giramondo, 2016) has won the 2017 Judith Wright Calanthe Poetry Prize.

Volumes of Kit Kelen's poetry have been published in Chinese, Portuguese, French, Italian, Spanish, Swedish, Indonesian and Filipino. His next English-language collection, *Poor Man's Coat – Hardanger Poems* is being published by University of Western Australia Press in 2018. Kit Kelen is Emeritus Professor of English at the University of Macau, where he taught Literature and Creative Writing for many years.

S. K. Kelen lives in the bush capital and enjoys hanging around the house, philosophically, and traveling. His most recent book is a volume of new and selected travel poems. *yonder blue wild*, published by Flying Island Books.

Dien Bien Phu: Dragon Rising, S. K. Kelen, (The Gioi, Hanoi, 1998 *Shimmerings*, S. K. Kelen (Five Island Press, 2000). *The Long Trudge: Earthly Delights*, S. K. Kelen (Pandanus: Canberra, 2006 Peril, *Rebel* no.3 May 2007.

Anne Kellas's *The White Room Poems* (Walleah Press) was shortlisted for the Margaret Scott Prize in the 2017 Tasmanian Premier's Literary awards. *Isolated States* (Cornford Press, 2001) and *Poems from Mt Moono* (Hippogriff, 1989) are represented along with new work in *The Netted Air* (Picaro Poets, 2018). Anne lives in Hobart where she teaches writing.

Jean Kent grew up in rural Queensland and now lives at Lake Macquarie, NSW. She is the author of eight books of poetry: the most recent are *The Hour of Silvered Mullet* (Pitt Street Poetry, 2015) and *Paris in my Pocket* (PSP, 2016). Her maternal grandfather was a Light Horseman in WWI.

Myra King lives in South Australia, her work has appeared in Rochford Street Review, Boston Literary Magazine, Orbis, and Heron's Nest. She has won the UK Global, the US Moon Prize and been shortlisted for many other awards. Myra's short story collection, *City Paddock*, and YA novels *The Journey of Velvet Brown* and *The Diaries of Velvet Brown*, have been published by Ginninderra Press.

Andy Kissane has published a novel, a book of short stories, *The Swarm*, and four books of poetry. *Radiance* (Puncher & Wattmann, 2014) was shortlisted for the Victorian and Western Australian Premier's Prizes and the Adelaide Festival Awards. He was the winner of the 2017 Tom Collins Prize for Poetry. http://andykissane.com

"Raking the Powder, 1943" was previously published in *Every Night They Dance* (Five Islands Press, 2000). "My Husband's Grave" was previously published in *Radiance* (Puncher & Wattmann, 2014).

komninos has been writing and performing poetry since 1979, earning his living as a performer and workshop facilitator since 1985. he has taught at university where he also pioneered computer based cyberpoetry. komninos graduated as a master of arts in creative writing in 1996 and taught at Griffith university gold coast from 1999 to 2007. komninos is now living in poetry friendly melbourne as a submerging artist.

Christopher Konrad is a Western Australian writer and has poems and short stories published in many journals and online. He has received many awards including winning the Glen Phillips Poetry Prize 2015 and Tom Collins Poetry Award 2009. His latest book, *Argot*, was published by Pomonal Publishing (2016).

Servet Kördeve is a language teacher from Istanbul with Bachelor of Arts in English Literature at Canakkale Onsekiz Mart University. While having written many poetic works yet to be published, he seeks to pursue a literary career focusing on poetry. Nowadays he does personal consultancy in professional matters and does editorship in English and in Swedish.

Yota Krili Published works: *Triptych: Poems,* (Owl Publishing Melbourne 2003), translation into Greek of the novel *Women of the Sun* (University Studio Press, Thessaloniki 2008), the trilogy Pathways to Freedom, novels: *Katavoles* (Pteroti House, Sydney 2013), *Kyparissomilo* (Pteroti House, Sydney 2014), *Cyclamino,* (Pteroti House, Sydney 2016), *Christina's Case:* play, (Pteroti House, Sydney 2016).

Mike Ladd has published nine books of poetry and prose, including the haibun *Karrawirra Parri, Walking the Torrens from Source to Sea.* His latest collection, *Invisible Mending,* was published by Wakefield Press in 2016. He was the founding producer and editor of *Poetica* on ABC Radio National.

Martin Langford has published seven books of poetry, the most recent of which is *Ground* (P&W, 2015). He is co-editor (with J. Beveridge, J. Johnson and D. Musgrave) of *Contemporary Australian Poetry* (Puncher and Wattmann, 2016). An essayist and critic, he is the poetry reviewer for Meanjin.

'Gallipoli' and 'The Kingfisher's Wings' were first published in *Ground* (P&W, 2015).

Katrina Larsen is a New Zealand poet who has previously been published in *Blackmail Press, Takahe* and *Poetry NZ.* When she is not being a mother and a teacher, she enjoys travelling and a good book.

Roland Leach has three collections of poetry, the latest *My Father's Pigs* published by Picaro Press. He is the proprietor of Sunline Press, which has published nineteen collections of poetry by Australian poets. His latest venture is *Cuttlefish,* a new magazine that includes art, poetry, flash fiction and short fiction. It is online at www.sunlinpress.com.au

Rozanna Lilley has published creative non-fiction and poetry in national newspapers and literary journals. Her writing has also been featured in Best Australian Essays (2013 and 2014) and Best Australian Poetry (2015). Her hybrid memoir *Do Oysters Get Bored? A Curious Life* (UWA Publishing) was released in April 2018.

Andrew Lindsay is a writer, performer and teacher. He has published two novels with Allen and Unwin, The Breadmaker's Carnival and The Slapping Man. He is a winner of the National Jazz Writing Competition, The Peter Blazey Fellowship, Radio National Books and Writing Short Story Competition, and the FAW (Vic) Jim Hamilton Award.

Ray Liversidge has written three books of poetry, *Obeying the Call, no suspicious circumstances: portraits of poets (dead), Oradour-sur-Glane,* a verse novel, *The Barrier Range,* and a chapbook, *The Divorce Papers.* His poems also featured in the book, *Triptych Poets: Issue One.* He has his own website at: www.poetray.wordpress.com

Earl Livings has published poetry and fiction in Australia and also Britain, Canada, the USA, and Germany. His work mainly focuses on nature, mythology and the sacred. He is currently working on a dark ages novel and his next poetry collection will be published in late 2018.

Kate Lumley is a Sydney-based writer. Kate has been published in *Studio, Australian Love Poems 2013* (Inkerman & Blunt) and *Prayers of a Secular World* (Inkerman & Blunt). She received a highly commended in the 2014 Adrien Abbott poetry prize and a highly commended in the 2014 Glen Phillips Poetry Prize.

Lorraine McGuigan Publications include *Quadrant, Eureka Street, Antipodes, Social Alternatives, Australian Love Poems anthology.* 20 years editor of *Poetry Monash.* Her collection, *What the Body Remembers,* shared 2nd in FAW Anne Elder Award. Interactive Press published her prizewinning ms *Wings of the Same Bird.*

'Uncle Mac's Leg' first published in *Wings of the Same Bird* (Interactive, 2009).

Jill McKeowen lives in Newcastle and her poems are published in several anthologies. She teaches academic writing at the University of Newcastle.

Jennifer Maiden has 27 books : 22 poetry, 5 novels. Among awards: 3 Slessors, 2 C. J. Dennis, overall Victorian Prize Literature, Christopher Brennan, 2 Melbourne Age Poetry Book, overall Melbourne Age Book of Year, ALS Gold Medal. Shortlisted Griffin. Poem here written for this, since published in JM's *Appalachian Fall* (Quemar Press).

Among Chris Mansell's latest publications are *Verge, Stung, Stung More, Spine Lingo,* and *Schadenvale Road. Seven Stations* (a song cycle with music by Andrew Batt-Rawden) was released by Hospital Hill on CD. Her site is chrismansell.com. She won the Queensland Premier's Award for Poetry, Amelia Chapbook Award (USA) and the Meanjin Dorothy Porter Poetry Prize and has been short-listed for the National Book Council Award and the NSW Premier's Award.

'the general becomes' previously appeared in *Verge* Chris Mansell (Wellsprung Productions, 2016). 'Some Wars' previously appeared in *The Beekeeper's War* (Wellsprung Productions, 2017).

Lorraine Marwood loves poetry as a form to convey narrative and emotion, simply and succinctly. Her latest verse novel will be published this year with UQP. *Star Jumps* a verse novel for children won the inaugural Prime Minister's Literature prize for children. She writes for both adults and children. www.lorrainemarwood.com

Geoffrey Moyle is the author of 2 books of poetry – *My Hands Are Your Hands* (self-published 2015) and *The Only Car On The Road* (self-published 2018). He is also a Cost Planner, spending most of his professional time consulting with Architects & their clients.

Norm Neill's poetry has appeared in journals, anthologies and newspapers, and he has read at festivals. His poems have been placed in the Fish Prize (Ireland) and Inner City Life competitions. He convenes a poetry workshop and has had 1000+ letters published in the *Sydney Morning Herald* and the *Australian*.

"aged four" appeared in *Blue Giraffe* 13.

K A Nelson is a Canberra poet who published her first collection, *Inlandia*, with Recent Work Press earlier this year. Her poems have been published, anthologised, and a few have won prizes. She is currently writing a memoir with poetry as part of postgraduate studies at the University of Canberra.

Gisela Sophia Nittel After completing a PhD in German Literature, she turned to writing poetry and memoir. Gisela has a poetry blog and is an active member of three poetry groups in Sydney. Her poems have been published in *Australian Poetry Journal, Going Down Swinging, Australian Poetry Collaboration* and *Yours&Mine*.

jenni nixon is a Sydney poet, performer – published 'café boogie' (interactive, 2004) *agenda!* (picaro, 2009) 'swimming underground' (Ginninderra, 2015). Widely published in small press anthologies include: *spineless wonders, first refuge, writing to the wire, not very quiet*.

A Bombardier on the Bus previously published: swimming underground 2015, Best Australian Poems 2009, Conversations from the Bottom of the Harbour 2009, Agenda! 2009. Read at the State funeral celebrating Hon. Tom Uren AC. Sydney Town Hall, February 2015. Broadcast on the ABC and iView.

Mark O'Flynn's most recent collection of poems is *Shared Breath*, (Hope Street Press, 2017). He has published a collection of short stories as well as four novels. His latest *The Last Days of Ava Langdon* (2016) was shortlisted for the 2017 Miles Franklin Award, the Prime Ministers

Literary Award, and was winner of the Voss Literary Award.

Sheryl Persson's poems have been published in journals, anthologies and educational publications in Australia and abroad and as a member of DiVerse, she has performed her work at galleries and museums. Sheryl is also the author of non-fiction books, including *Smallpox, Syphilis and Salvation*.

Reneé Pettitt-Schipp lived on Christmas Island and the Cocos (Keeling) Islands for three years, inspiring her first collection of poetry, *The Sky Runs Right Through Us*, shortlisted for the Dorothy Hewett manuscript prize and released by UWA Publishing in February 2018. Reneé currently lives in karri country in Western Australia's deep south. http://www.reneepettittschipp.com.au/

The poems were first published in *borderlands* e-journal 11(3).

Vaughan Rapatahana is widely published across several genres. He won the inaugural Proverse Poetry prize in 2016, the same year his collection Atonement was nominated for a National Book Award in Philippines. His latest collection is *ternion* (erbacce-press, Liverpoool, UK). He lives in three countries a year — New Zealand; Hong Kong; Philippines.

Mark Roberts is a Sydney based writer and critic. Along with Linda Adair he edits P76 magazine and Rochford Street Press/Review. His work has been widely published in journals and anthologies around the world. His collection of poems, *Concrete Flamingos*, was published by Island Press in 2017.

Robyn Rowland's newest books are *Mosaics from the Map* (Doire Press, Galway, 2018) and *This Intimate War: Gallipoli/*Çanakkale *1915* — İçli *Dışlı Bir Savaş: Gelibolu/*Çanakkale *1915*, Turkish translations Mehmet Ali Çelikel (Five Islands, 2015; Spinifex, 2018).

Acknowledgement: *This Intimate War Gallipoli/*Çanakkale *1915* — İçli *Dışlı Bir Savaş: Gelibolu/*Çanakkale *1915*, Turkish translations Mehmet Ali Çelikel (Spinifex, 2018; Five Islands; Bilge Kultur Sanat, Turkey; 2015)

Brenda Saunders is an artist and writer of Wiradjuri and British descent. She has published three collections of poetry and her work appears in many anthologies and journals such as *Australian Poetry Journal*, *Overland*, *StylusLit*, *Southerly* and *Best Australian Poems 2013 and 2015*. Brenda reviews for *Verity La*, *Mascara* and *Plumwood Mountain*.

Kerri Shying is a poet and sculptor of Chinese and Wiradjuri family who lives in Newcastle. Her book of poems *sing out when you want me*, from Flying Island/ASM/Cerberus Press, was published in 2018. Her forebear was the grandfather of the first Chinese-Australian serviceman.

Erin Signal is a Kwaussie who recently moved from Wellington to Melbourne. She is pursuing a love of writing poetry after a career as a newspaper subeditor came to its end and is working as a private car hire driver. Rowan is her nephew.

Alex Skovron is the author of six poetry collections, a prose novella and a book of short stories, *The Man who Took to his Bed* (2017). His latest volume of poetry, *Towards the Equator: New & Selected Poems* (2014), was shortlisted in the Prime Minister's Literary Awards. He lives in Melbourne.

A.T.Spathis is a scientist and engineer who also writes poetry, fiction, and non-fiction. During the period of the Arab spring, he won two poetry prizes from the Bibliotheca Alexandrina in Egypt. He has managed to tame the art of self-publishing for himself and other writers.

Malcolm St Hill lives in Newcastle and is a poet, reviewer and independent researcher focused on the literary memory of the Great War. He has presented internationally on the literature of the Australian light-horsemen and at the National Library of Australia, on Australian soldier-poets.

Sarah St Vincent Welch is a Canberra-based writer. She grew up in Sydney in a house full of WWI relics that belonged to her grandfather. His poetry and mythology books sparked her imagination. He was a doctor, officer, artist, cartographer, and photographer. His family wish they could know more about him.

Linda Stevenson is a Melbourne (Australia) poet; the content of her poems is primarily world environment and issues of equity in society. Her latest collection is a Chapbook *The Tipping Point*, containing powerful activist ecopoems. Her work is also currently published in local and international literary journals and special interest magazines.

John-Karl Stokes is known internationally as one of Australia's most courageous, innovative and interesting of writers. He's won, been shortlisted or long-listed for many international prizes and contributed to many journals and anthologies. Major collections include: *A River in the Dark (Five Islands)* and *Fire in the Afternoon (Halstead Press)*. www.johnkarlstokes.com

Bhupen Thakker Obsessed by colour Light Blue / Winner of NSW Poetry Sprint/ Highly Commended CJ Dennis awards/ Three time State Finalist in Australian Poetry Slam/2016 Winner Australian Multilingual Slam/A blog post number 2 in the world/ Day Job International Finance/Novel "A New Gandhi, a New Monet and many others" emerging. http://bhupenthakker.blogspot.com.au

Willem Tibben came from Holland to Australia in 1954 and grew up on dairy farms. He worked in the NSW Public Service for 43 years and retired in 2007. He has published four books: *near myths* (1986); *the conscious moment* (1996); *the fascination of what's simple* (2005); *suburban veneer* (2017).

Richard Tipping's first books were *Soft Riots, Domestic Hardcore* and *Nearer by Far* (UQP, 1972-1986), the latest are Tommy Ruff (Press-Press, 2014) and *Instant History* (Flying Island, 2017). Experimenting with concrete poetry since 1967, he drifted into the art world and stayed there, making textual objects and disturbing the templates of public signage. www.richardtipping.com

Rose van Son is a prize-winning West Australian poet. She has been published in several journals including *Westerly, Rabbit, Cordite* and *Blood Orange Review (USA)*. She was Poetry Guest at the Perth Poetry Festival 2015; her collections include *Sandfire, Three in the Campagna* (a collaboration) and *Three Owls and a Crescent Moon*. Her new collection is ready for publication.

Saba Vasefi is a poet, academic, multi-award winning artist, filmmaker and PhD candidate in feminist cinema studies at Macquarie University. She is the director of the Sydney International Women's Poetry & Arts Festival. She was twice a judge for the Sedigheh Dolatabadi Book Prize for the Best Book on Women's Literature and Women's Issues.

Lyn Vellins is a Sydney-based published poet. She ran a monthly poetry reading group, 'RhiZomic' until 2017, and was on the committee of many reputed publications and on several editorial committees whilst at Sydney University. Her first collection of poetry, A Fragile Transcendence, was published by Picaro Press in July, 2012.

Rob Walker has six poetry collections, including *tropeland* (Five Islands, 2015) and *Original Clichés* (Ginninderra Press, 2016) with hundreds of poems in journals in UK, US and Australia. www.rob-walkerpoet.com

'Anzacs' published in *War Music and other poems – a selection by South Australian poets, Anzac Day 2015* (Garron)

Chris Wallace-Crabbe is a leading Melbourne poet and Professor

Emeritus in literature at the University of Melbourne. His latest book is *Afternoon in the Central Nervous System* (Braziller: New York, 2015). His uncle Keith was killed at Gallipoli in 1915.

James Walton has been published in many anthologies and journals. He lives in an isolated farming community in South Gippsland. He has been a librarian, a farm labourer, a cattle breeder, and mostly a public-sector union official. His collection *The Leviathan's Apprentice* was published in 2015.

Leonie Wellard is in love with poetry and has been writing it (on and off) for most of her life. She has been published in Cordite and various anthologies. She is currently writing her first verse novel.

Peter J Wells is a poet and writer based in Newcastle. He has been published in local and online. Shortlisted for the UOC Vice Chancellors International Poetry Prize in 2015. He makes ends meet by working as an Engineer.

Les Wicks has toured widely and seen publication in over 350 different magazines, anthologies & newspapers across 28 countries in 13 languages. *His 13th book of poetry is Getting By   Not Fitting In* (Island, 2016). http://leswicks.tripod.com/lw.htm

The Redactions previously published in *Cordite*.

Paul Williamson has published poems on a broad range of topics in magazines and e-zines in Australia, the US, Canada and the UK – including in Quadrant, Cordite and Short and Twisted. His collections are *The DNA Bookshelf, Moments from Red Hill, To the Spice Islands* and *Edge of Southern Bright* (Ginninderra, 2017); www.paulwilliamson.net.

'Other War Damage' has been published in *Edge of Southern Bright* (2017).

Georgina Woods is an environmentalist and poet living and working on Awabakal and Worimi land in Newcastle, New South Wales. She has a PhD in English Literature from Newcastle University and earns her living as an environmental advocate.